lovedecisions

lovedecisions

A father talks with his daughter about lasting relationships

Dr. Donald Harvey

W PUBLISHING GROUP™

www.wpublishinggroup.com

A Division of Thomas Nelson, Inc.
www.ThomasNelson.com

Published by W Publishing Group, a Division of Thomas Nelson, Inc., P. O. Box 141000, Nashville, Tennessee 37214.

Unless otherwise indicated, Scripture verses are quoted from the Revised Standard Version of the Bible, copyright © 1952 (2nd edition, 1971) by the Division of Christian Education of the National Council of the Churches of Christ in the USA. Used by permission. All rights reserved.

Other Scripture passages are from the following sources:

The King James Version of the Bible (KJV).

The Holy Bible, New International Version (NIV). Copyright © 1973, 1978, 1984, International Bible Society. Used by permission of Zon-dervan Bible Publishers.

The New American Standard Bible (NASB), © 1960, 1977 by the Lockman Foundation.

The New English Bible (NEB), copyright © 1961, 1970, The Delegates of the Oxford University Press and the Syndics of the Cambridge University Press, Tyndale House, Cambridge, United Kingdom.

Names of persons and details of their stories shared in this volume have been changed to protect their privacy. Some illustrations are composites.

"We went from zero to love in nothin' flat" in chapter 5 is from the song "Love Happens Like That" by Aaron G. Baerker Sr., Anthony Smith, Ron Harbin, © copyright 1997. Blind Sparrow Music/BMI (admin. by ICG)/O-Tex Music/BMI/Kim Williams Music/ASCAP/Sony/Cross Keys Publishing Co., Inc./ASCAP/Notes to Music/ASCAP/Maverick Music/ASCAP. All rights reserved. Used by permission.

Library of Congress Cataloging-in-Publication Data

Harvey, Donald R. (Donald Reid), 1948–
    lovedecisions : a father talks with his daughter about lasting relationships / Donald Harvey.
    p. cm.
    ISBN 0-8499-1793-X (hardcover)
    1. Man–woman relationships. 2. Man–woman relatinships—Religious aspects—Christianity. 3. Love. 4. Love—Religious aspects—Christianity. I. Title: Father talks with his daughter about lasting relationships. II. Title.

HQ801.H3523   2003
306.7–dc21

                                       2003004636

Printed in the United States of America
03 04 05 06 07 BVG 9 8 7 6 5 4 3 2 1

To Jan and Paige,

the two women in my life.
Each in her own way has
taught me the meaning of love—
and to love deeply.

Contents

Contents

Introduction: The Story of **love**decisions

IN A REAL SENSE, I've been talking to my daughter, Paige, about love and lasting relationships for almost twenty-five years. Every time I kissed her mother, Jan, or apologized to Jan when something I had said needlessly hurt her feelings, or gave up something that was important to me so that Jan could have or do something that was important to her, or risked the safety found in keeping my thoughts and feelings to myself by disclosing something personal and private, or shared Jan's times of both joy and pain—every time I did these things, I was talking to Paige about love. For good or bad, nothing has spoken louder to Paige than my marriage to her mother.

And every time I was there for Paige—whether in sacrificing my needs for hers or in listening to her stories, really hearing what she was trying to say, understanding that she was different than I and appreciating it, respecting her as a person of worth uniquely created and loved by God, bringing her to His throne—every time I did these things, I was talking to Paige about love.

In these ways, I have modeled love to Paige for many years. This has affected not only who she is but who she will seek as her mate. I'm a therapist. I know things like this. I also know my influence has not ended just because Paige is "all grown up" now. Developmentally, Paige is at a place now—more than ever before—where my words, and not just my life, can also be of influence.

I realize that not everyone is able to respond to words in the same manner. Sometimes our ability to hear is impacted by who is doing the talking. So I have to ask myself, *Have I earned the right by deed to say what needs to be said?* At other times, our ability to hear is impacted by our own level of emotional well-being. We are created as both *intellectual* and *emotional* beings—we think and we feel. As such, there is a ratio combining these two aspects that depicts our ability to listen. Those of us who function with a big *I* and a little *e* (I/e)—the rational folks—seem to benefit most from hearing words. And those of us who function with a big *E* and a little *i* (E/i)—the emotionally driven folks—benefit least from them. But no matter where we fall in these ratios, none of us is completely beyond the influence of words.

I haven't been perfect as a husband or a father, but I believe I've earned the right to say some things about love and what it takes to successfully build a lasting relationship. And although Paige has already made the break from youth to adulthood, she is still in the process of making what I call *lovedecisions*. She is "ready" to listen. In this book I share the things I want to *say*, but more importantly, these are the crucial things I want Paige—and other young women who are considering lifetime relationships—to *know* about love.

SOME UNIQUE FEATURES OF THIS BOOK

Lovedecisions is like no other book I have written and has several unique qualities. The title itself is unusual. Obviously, *lovedecisions* is not a real word. Every time I type it into the computer a red squiggly line appears under it, alerting me to my typo. But it so captures the essence, challenge, and task of the single young-adult state that it just leapt off the page as I was writing it. So I have kept it. This book is written for those in the lovedecisions phase of life.

Another unique quality is the amount of time I have been working on this book. It has required seven years to complete. I began writing *lovedecisions,* and involving Paige in the editing process, when she left for college. There were things I wanted her to know about love, and this was a way for me to say them. I continued writing as she took the next adult step and entered the world of work and career.

During those seven years, she has dated several young men—some seriously, some not. If you could see how beautiful she is, you would understand why! But that is as it should be; we learn a lot in relationships, both short and long. Jokingly, I have accused Paige of "keeping me in content." As of this writing, she is still in the lovedecisions phase—still single and unattached, and still making good decisions about love.

Finally, most books are not written with e-mails preceding each chapter. I have chosen to use the e-mails for two reasons: I wanted to quickly and succinctly identify the focus of each chapter, and this was a way of doing that. But also, I wanted to bring a little warmth to the content of the chapters that follow.

Paige and I have grown closer as we have discussed her

relationships and developed this book. Of course, the names and circumstances have been altered to protect the privacy of the people who have been Paige's friends and acquaintances over the years. But other than that, these e-mails are composites of actual communications we have had. Sometimes we talked by phone, sometimes through e-mail, and sometimes face to face on those occasions when she was either home from school or I had made arrangements to travel through Oklahoma on business. More recently, as she has become a career woman in Nashville, we have had opportunities to share lunch or dinner. These have become precious times in a dad's life. I will be forever indebted for what being a dad to Paige has meant to me.

Dr. Donald Harvey

Dear Paige

To: Paige@College.com
From: Dad@HarveyHome.com
Subject: You're growing up!

Dear Paige,

You have been such a bright spot in my life. I've watched you grow from an infant totally dependent upon your mother and me for your every need to a beautiful young woman whose life seems to be defined by the term *independent*. This experience has been both emotional and educational for me. We have laughed together—and cried. And, of course, there is that special bond we share—the love of a good spy movie.

Think of all of the things I would have missed if you hadn't been in my life. There's been that progressive movement in transportation—from trikes to bikes to cars. Teaching you to drive was an experience I

To: Paige@College.com
From: Dad@HarveyHome.com
Subject: You're growing up!

will never forget (and one that I would not want to repeat!). Our family vacations and trips have given me a second childhood. Your love of the sun and water has taken me to three coasts. We've picked up seashells, watched the whales, and dodged surfers together. Then there were the extracurricular activities—the lessons and recitals and watching you cheerlead. And can we forget my introduction to the world of acting when supporting you in your modeling career led me to being a part of a television commercial? Most importantly, I would have missed out on all your love—progressively expressed from "Daddy, I love you so much" to "Dad, you're the bomb" and most recently to "Dad, I respect you more than you know."

It seemed like you would always be my little girl—always looking to me for advice, always wanting me to help you accomplish something. But time has a way of crushing our fantasies. Now I cry just watching television commercials that end with the father

To: Paige@College.com
From: Dad@HarveyHome.com
Subject: You're growing up!

giving his daughter away at her wedding. I know one day that will be me. I don't think I'm ready yet . . .

I remember when you first started to date—at least, the "official" dates—when the boys came by the house and actually picked you up versus your meeting by chance at the mall. Being a marriage and family therapist, I know how to make people feel at ease, and I also know how to make them feel uncomfortable. I wanted to meet each young man in person—and was never very interested in making him feel at ease. It was OK with me if your dates always felt a little intimidated.

All of that changed when you left for college. Your mother told me one day, "You know, you're going to have to be nicer to the boys Paige dates from now on. Each one could be a potential son-in-law."

I knew what she was saying. The game had changed. You had done more than graduate from high school. You had moved into the

To: Paige@College.com
From: Dad@HarveyHome.com
Subject: You're growing up!

time in your life when your list of "special people" would include more than just your family; you had moved into the time for making *lovedecisions*. The importance of your dating relationships had been kicked up a notch. Each new guy was now a potential husband.

This is an important time in your life. The relationships you enter now are more significant. Your decisions are more lasting. When you were younger, I had more influence on the decisions you made. You were my little girl. Though a part of that will never change, you are almost totally on your own now.

Paige, I love you very much, and I have a lot of confidence in who you are becoming. More and more, I have learned to trust your judgment. But letting go isn't easy for me. There's still a part of me that wishes I could make some of those decisions for you—especially when the decisions involve relationships. I know I can't. But even though these are decisions you must make on your own, I

To: Paige@College.com
From: Dad@HarveyHome.com
Subject: You're growing up!

still want to have an influence. So as you make the transition into adulthood—and as you work through the process of making your own lovedecisions—these are the things I want you to know about love.

You will always be my girl—and I will always love you.

Dad

PART 1

WHAT YOU NEED TO KNOW
ABOUT LOVE BEFORE YOU GET STARTED

2

You Will Have to Leave Home

To: Paige@SummerJob.com
Fom: Dad@HarveyHome.com
Subject: Leaving home

Dear Paige,

Your mother and I have been talking about how different you seem this summer compared with last summer before you went off to college. It has occurred to us that by our seeing you only occasionally now we see more clearly the changes that are taking place in your life. The gaps between our time together actually make these changes more distinct. There is an air about you—a sophistication—that wasn't there when you left for college a year ago. I guess you are really growing up.

You are in the stage of life when you "leave home"—and when you learn that leaving home is a whole lot more about emotional

To: Paige@SummerJob.com
From: Dad@HarveyHome.com
Subject: Leaving home

separation than it is about geography. Change is what this stage is all about.

You're supposed to be making the creative leap from dependence to independence— from being reliant upon us to being reliant upon yourself. You are supposed to leave us. I guess that's what we're seeing you do.

There's something else I have noticed. Though you are "leaving," you have not totally "left." I can tell this by several things. The first is the four-hundred-dollar long-distance phone bills we've accrued in the past year. Another is the drain on my bank account. Scientists tell us there's a great black hole somewhere in space. Anything that gets too close to this hole, they speculate, will be sucked into it. Actually, I think this great black hole is located seven hundred miles west of Nash-ville in Oklahoma. At least something out there keeps sucking all my money away. I will know you have really left home when the drain on my bank account ceases.

To: Paige@SummerJob.com
From: Dad@HarveyHome.com
Subject: Leaving home

All of this tells me that leaving home is a process. It's a lot like making the trip back to school, Paige. You don't just hop in your car in Nashville, start the engine, and then immediately arrive in Oklahoma. There are stops and starts along the way, towns and cities to pass through, and even occasional detours to be encountered—all en route to your final destination. I guess you won't leave home in one giant step, either. I know you will gradually "wean" yourself away from us. But it will be the result of many small steps—some forward and others backward—until finally you are on your own.

Living with you this summer has been different from last summer. It was supposed to be. It will be even more different next summer. Who knows? You may even decide not to come home at all! You may choose instead to go to Europe for that special "educational" experience or pursue an internship in another city or just stay in Oklahoma and work so you can be close to the friends you've made in college. Next summer is still a long

> **To:** Paige@SummerJob.com
> **From:** Dad@HarveyHome.com
> **Subject:** Leaving home
>
> way off. But even to entertain these possibilities tells me you are leaving. I will miss you when you are gone. But it's what you are supposed to do, it's what you need to do, and it's what we have raised you to do.
>
> Thinking of you when you aren't here,
>
> Dad

SO YOU THINK YOU'RE READY TO GET MARRIED

I was meeting with a group of engaged couples, all of them college students in the lovedecisions stage of life and all very interested in knowing more about marriage. We were talking about relationships that last. Everyone in the group was "in love," and as expected whenever youth and love are combined, a special electricity sizzled through the air. Each of our sessions had been marked with high energy, lots of positive emotions, and plenty of conversation.

We had already discussed how marriage is a complex union—not as simple as some might think—and we had spent a lot of time identifying some of the characteristics that make up healthy relationships. Then I asked my couples this question: "Have you *really* left home?"

All of a sudden, the conversation came to a grinding halt. And *poof!* The electric atmosphere disappeared, too! What had caused the change? I quickly scanned their faces for a possible clue. Was the question too personal? As I tried to interpret their expressions, I discerned that the common response did not seem to be embarrassment but confusion, as if they were asking, *Why would he ask such a crazy question—one with such an obvious answer?* After all, they were college students who would be graduating in just a few months. They lived in dorms and apartments, obviously not under the watchful eye of Mom and Dad. And they lived a long way from home—some as much as several thousand miles. So they were confused. Yet I stuck with my question and again asked: "Have you really left home?"

I pressed the question because I believe the answer is very important. It has great implications for whether a marriage will ultimately be successful. I also believe Scripture supports the importance of this question and has a lot to tell us, not only about the question, but also about the answer.

THE BIBLICAL MODEL

God's design for marriage is given to us very early in Scripture. Genesis 2:24 records, "Therefore a man *leaves* his father and his mother and *cleaves* to his wife, and they become one flesh" (my italics). Frequently referred to as the "leave-and-cleave passage," this verse presents two distinct, though related, concepts. A person *leaves* (detaches), and a person *cleaves* (attaches). Though I'll spend some time in later chapters discussing what it actually means for a person to *cleave* in a relationship, what is important to the question that I asked my premarital group is the *leave* portion of this verse.

By design, you are to leave home. Scripture clearly connects the two distinct concepts of detaching and attaching because you cannot accomplish one unless you have successfully accomplished the other.

You are supposed to leave *and* cleave.

You have to leave *before* you can cleave.

You have to leave *in order* to cleave.

The overriding principle from Scripture for anyone thinking about marriage is this: You are not ready to *attach* until you have first *detached.* This is not a *compatibility* issue—but a *marriageability* issue. You are not ready to marry anyone (you are not *marriageable*)—regardless of how well you "fit" together (which is a *compatibility* issue)—until you have truly left home.

"SO, HAVE YOU *REALLY* LEFT HOME?"

As I continued to ask my premarital couples this question, they all continued to answer yes—for a while. But after I explained the leave-and-cleave process, they were not so sure. I could tell they had some doubts because they were saying things like, "Yes, I think I have," and "I thought I had, but now I'm not totally sure." What made them hesitant was that they were having a hard time coming up with any real *proof* to back up their yes answers. They needed evidence and finally decided I was asking the wrong question. They suggested a better question would be, "How do you know if you've really left home? Where's the proof?" Changing the question like this was a good leap because it enabled the couples to move away from simply making guesses to actually looking at the facts.

Before attempting to do the hard part, identifying the indications that they had really left home, they decided to do the easy part, identifying some things that are *not* indications. The first they agreed on was *age*. Though age may tell you when you're *supposed* to leave home, it's not by itself an indication that you've actually done it. You can be thirty years old and still be tied to home. Another factor they agreed on was *being in college*. Sure, there are responsibilities that go with being in college. And oftentimes you have to geographically leave home to get there. But everyone agreed that being away from home is not the same as leaving home. A final area of agreement was *marriage*. You'd like to think that getting married meant you had left home. But we've all seen too many contradictions of that supposition.

Though age, being in college, or even being married does not assure you that you've left home, there are other things you can look to as indications that this has been accomplished. Assessing whether you've left home does not have to be left to guesswork. You can *know*.

HOW TO KNOW YOU'VE REALLY LEFT HOME

There are actually several factors I look to in deciding whether you have really left home. But the most important seems to be *the role your parents play in the decisions you make*. When I suggested to my group of engaged couples that they had not yet left home if they continued to allow their parents to unduly influence their decisions, I got a wide range of responses.

On one extreme was the girl who told how she had bought a car completely on her own. She shopped around, looking at a bunch of models on several lots. After selecting what she thought was the best deal, she worked out her own financing and drove off with her new car. This was all done without any consultation from her parents. Her story prompted more confusion and some concerned responses like, "But I value my parents' advice. Does this mean I haven't left home?"

Let me help clarify the confusion. Whenever I'm dealing with the issue of your parents' influence on your life, my concern is always with the *degree* of their influence. Let's face it: Your parents are always going to influence your life—and that's not necessarily a bad thing. They can give you a lot of good input. But the real question becomes, Is it just input, or is it more than that? Do your parents overly influence (or control) your decisions, or are they merely providing you with helpful information you then use in your own decision-making process? *The* difference makes *all* the difference because overinfluence is an example of dependency—and an indication that you haven't yet left home. A *dependent you* will do what they want you to do because you don't want to cross them (or disappoint them or make them angry, etc.). But an *independent you* will accept their input as helpful data. You will consider their advice along with anything else you find helpful. And after due deliberation, you will make your own decision, regardless of what others thought was best. That's what independent adults who have left home do.

ARE YOU FOOLING YOURSELF?

Sometimes it's easy to see that you haven't completely left home. You readily see how you're still more concerned with what your parents think is best instead of what you think. But in some situations dependency is not so easy to see. Sometimes you're still unduly influenced, and you just don't know it. This is the case when you confuse leaving with geography, cutting yourself off emotionally, or rebelling.

Geography

I have spoken with adults who were so dissatisfied with their family that they moved thousands of miles in order to get away from them. They thought geography was the answer—that they could move far enough away to get away from their influence. Boy, were they wrong! Geography alone will never change the influence our family has on our life. Emotional bonds are tenacious, and your family's influence can cross many miles. If you're counting on geography to make the break from home, you need to rethink your solution.

Cutting yourself off emotionally

Others try to make the break by "emotionally" putting parents out of their lives. They may live in the same town but because of bad past experiences have nothing to do with their parents, bottling up the hurt feelings. They just don't talk anymore. They think cutting themselves off like this changes things. Again, it doesn't. The hurt is still there—and so is the influence. There's an old line that says, "The people you hate control your life." That's the way it is with bitterness. It always has a way of seeping out.

Rebelling

Rebels think they will show their independence by doing something that is different from what their parents would do. I'm not necessarily talking about doing bad things. But the issue always boils down to *why* you do what you do. Deciding to go to a different church than your parents doesn't make you a rebel. But

17

if you decide to switch churches just to show them how independent you are rather than because you genuinely prefer another congregation or denomination, that's another matter. Your decision is still based more on what they're thinking than on what you're thinking.

THE PROOF THAT YOU'VE LEFT HOME

When you have truly left home, you will demonstrate independence versus dependence—you will *act* versus *react*. And your decisions will have more to say about you than about other people. The bottom line will always be, "This is what *I* think is the best thing for me to do," and you will act accordingly. If, instead, your behavior is a reaction to others, then maybe (you guessed it) you still haven't left and there's still some work to do before you're ready to make any real lovedecisions.

Leaving home is not as simple as it sounds. It isn't just a by-product of age. Nor is it always indicated by a change in address. It's a process—one that requires many steps and encounters many interferences. Still, it is not only an accomplishable goal but one that must be attained before you are ready to make any significant lovedecisions. Assess yourself and your relationships. Have you made the break from home and dependence to self-sufficiency and independence? Are you somewhere "in process"? Or are you still clearly tied to your parents? The following worksheet may help you answer that question.

QUESTIONS TO CONSIDER:
HAVE YOU *REALLY* LEFT HOME?

1. What kind of influence do your parents have on the decisions you make right now?
   a. When it gets down to it, I have little say in any area of my life.
   b. Though I make some decisions, I still yield to my parents on the big issues.
   c. Though my parents may offer their opinions about the things I do, I am at a place in life where I make and take full responsibility for my own decisions.

2. If your parents were absolutely opposed to something you really thought was good to do, how willing would you be to do it anyway?
   a. Not in this lifetime.
   b. I'd give it a lot of thought, but I'd probably end up doing what they wanted rather than disappointing (crossing, hurting, etc.) them.
   c. I'd give their input due deliberation, but ultimately I'd do what I thought was best.

3. To what extent do you still rely on your parents for financial support?
   a. I regularly depend on them for money.
   b. They're helping me through college, but I plan to be independent after I graduate.
   c. I'm self-sufficient.

4. How content are you when you're not in a significant relationship?
   a. I feel desperate and alone. I can't stand to be without someone in my life.
   b. Sometimes I feel OK, but mostly I just feel lonely.
   c. I enjoy being in a relationship, but I also enjoy being by myself. Until Mr. Right comes along, I am content to be by myself, spend time with friends, and place my energies in worthy activities.

Interpreting your responses

If the *c* choices best describe your life, then congratulations! It sounds like you've successfully left home and are ready to make significant lovedecisions. On the other hand, if you had any *a* or *b* responses, there's still some work for you to do.

Also, if you're in a significant relationship, how do you think your boyfriend would answer the same set of questions? You might want to check, because he needs to be ready, too.

3

What *Is* Will *Be*

To: Paige@SummerJob.com
From: Dad@HarveyHome.com
Subject: What's really going on?

Dear Paige,

It was good to hear your voice this morning. You seemed to be a lot cheerier than the last time we talked. I guess the change in mood has something to do with how you and Brad are once again on speaking terms. I know that being at odds with your boyfriend can get you down.

A part of me would say I'm glad you and Brad made up. This seems to make you happy, and you know I always want you to be happy. There's another part of me that's not so sure. It seems that lately a lot of your happiness is closely connected to how you and Brad are getting along at that particular time. Maybe your happiness is too closely

To: Paige@SummerJob.com
From: Dad@HarveyHome.com
Subject: What's really going on?

related to Brad—and maybe your getting back together is not that great an idea after all.

I guess what really concerns me as your dad, Paige, is that this isn't the first time you and Brad have had the same kind of argument. And the way it looks to me, I don't think it's going to be the last. Arguing seems to have become a very real part of your daily routine. A pattern has developed. It's the presence of this pattern—the fact that what's going on happens again and again—that concerns me most. It doesn't look to me as if you and Brad think the same way about a lot of things.

I know it's easy to make up and just "forget" about whatever it was that started the disagreement. But patterns like this are red flags for any relationship. It's one thing to occasionally disagree over something. But when disagreement becomes repetitive, it's a different matter altogether.

To: Paige@SummerJob.com
From: Dad@HarveyHome.com
Subject: What's really going on?

I think it would be helpful for you to step back from the relationship a little and ask yourself, *What's really going on here? Why can't we get past this?* I know you've probably already asked yourself these questions because you've always been a discerning person. But maybe it's time to ask the questions again, to look squarely at the problem and let wisdom and maturity rise above the emotions of this relationship. And let me just say that I know it's not the easiest and certainly not the most fun thing to do. So call me if you want to talk through some of this. I'm all for supporting AT&T stockholders!

Ever the realist,

Dad

IS THERE A PATTERN?

Whenever I'm observing the behavior of others, I try not to jump to quick conclusions. I've learned that if you watch someone long enough you can see him or her do just about anything. So I operate on the principle of *incident* versus *pattern*. An *incident* is a behavior that occurs once or only rarely whereas a *pattern* is a behavior that occurs repeatedly. It's patterns that tell me a lot about people. So when I see something happening a lot—when I see a negative pattern—I know it's time for me to get concerned.

It was a pattern that caught my attention with Dave and Pam. Some couples come for premarital counseling with no agenda at all. They just know it's the wise thing to do. Others come because of a specific problem. That was the case with Dave and Pam. There had been an "incident" about church: Dave wanted to go one place and Pam another. How were they going to solve their dilemma? This is one of those types of problems where there isn't necessarily a right or wrong answer. The important thing isn't where they go, but how they reach their solution. So I was interested in seeing just how they'd manage to do this.

It didn't take long to see that they had a bigger problem than just deciding where they were going to go to church. Dave made that clear when he said, "God has told *me* where *we* ought to go to church—but Pam just won't listen to me."

I guess I wouldn't have thought this was all that alarming if where to attend church had been the only thing that God had told Dave. But as they shared the history of their relationship, the phrase "God has told me" occurred over and over again. And what God was telling Dave always had implications for Pam. God told Dave where Pam ought to work, who her friends should be, how she ought to be spending her time. (She was supposed to be spending more of her time with Dave.) The list went on and on. And whenever Pam disagreed with Dave, he told her she was disobeying God. What emerged was a pattern.

THE REAL PROBLEM

The real problem for Dave and Pam wasn't going to be found in the *content* of their disagreements. Nor would it be found in what God was supposedly telling Dave, or in what Pam was supposedly refusing to hear. The real struggle in their relationship was something far more basic and crucial. It was over *power.* Who was going to determine what Pam should do? In Dave's mind, it was he; it was his God-given right to be in charge of her every move. He had spent the past two years trying to convince Pam of the certainty of his position.

I really don't think God had much to do with Dave's behavior. Wherever they fell on the continuum of what a "Bible marriage" was supposed to look like—whether it's composed of a *hierarchy* with one person having more to say about things than the other or it's composed of two partners who are in *mutual submission* to one another—Dave's desire was for neither one of those options. Dave wanted complete domination. His and Pam's problem was not a religious issue; it was a personality issue. His personality dictated that Dave needed to be in control. He was driven by his own insecurities. If he was not in total control, he felt very uncomfortable. And for two years, though the content of their arguments might have changed, the struggle had not. It was merely a new verse of the same old song.

THE GREAT MYTH: THINGS WILL BE DIFFERENT

Having been a marital therapist for more than twenty-five years, I've had the chance to talk to many couples who were thinking about getting married. And I've learned a lot from these "nearly weds." But one of the most important truths I have learned about the lovedecisions phase of life has not come from nearly weds but from marital veterans—couples who have come for counseling after being married ten, twenty, or even thirty years and longer. And what is this important truth I've learned?

What *is* will *be*.

If something is occurring during the dating phase of your relationship, you can count on it being there long after the wedding ceremony.

This is a simple truth—but it's not an *easy* truth. It's easier to believe *things will be different*. This thinking is what I call the *great myth*. Believing this myth allows you to continue doing exactly what you want to do, what feels good. You don't have to change a thing.

Overlooking the truth and believing the myth that things will be different supports the old saying, "Love is blind." Now, I don't believe that love is necessarily blind. But I do think you can let passion and emotion cloud your judgment. Still, no matter how you choose to overlook reality, it does not change the facts. If something is there—if it is in your relationship now—it will continue to be there. What *is* will *be*. And overlooking the truth always has a consequence.

THREE WAYS WE AVOID REALITY

I am convinced that we really don't like reality very much. You see, the simple truth is this: *Reality is.*

Reality is not what we wish, want, or hope it to be. It just is. But we prefer to believe myths like *Things are really not as they appear* (though they are), *Things will be different than they are* (though they won't), or *I will change things in the future* (though you can't). We want what we want so we try to change reality into something other than what it is—we try to make it what we want—instead of accepting it for what it is. This never works. But we go on fooling ourselves anyway.

The three most common ways people in the lovedecisions phase of life attempt to avoid reality are denial, magical thinking, and taking on a project. Let me describe these three efforts in futility.

Denial

Denial is *the act of refusing to see reality.* Your mother sees the problems. Your brother sees the problems. Your sister, roommate, friends—everyone in the world sees the problems. Everyone, that is, but you. To you, there is no problem.

In your mind, it makes no difference what everyone else sees. Others simply "do not understand." They don't see the qualities you see. They don't know the real person. Whether it's a case of "love is blind" or some other malady, when you're in denial you refuse to recognize what is happening.

Magical thinking

Magical thinking is *manipulating reality by believing something's going to happen that will magically transform your situation.* With magical thinking you do not deny that a problem exists. So that's at least a step in the right direction. You admit there are things you would like to see changed. But you believe something will happen to cause these undesirable behaviors to magically disappear.

Usually the marriage ceremony is seen as the magical event. There's just something about that ceremony!

The truth is there is nothing magical about a ceremony. All that getting married changes is the *intensity* of your relationship. If you think things with your boyfriend are difficult now, just wait until you're married. They'll get worse.

Taking on a project

In taking on a project (just like with magical thinking), you recognize that problems do exist between you and your boyfriend. You're not in denial. So your error isn't your failure to recognize the problems but your solution for them. You mistakenly believe that once the two of you are married things will be different because *you can change things.*

You believe, *I will change him into what I want him to be.* Or you may have an even nobler attitude, thinking you can change him into what he "ought" to be. Either way, you believe that once you are together—once he's "yours"—things will be different. This kind of thinking has disaster written all over it.

THE ART OF LOOKING AT THE PRESENT TENSE

Whenever I am involved in premarital counseling, I am guided by one simple rule: *The problems that are going to be in the marriage are already there.* So I look for the "present tense" of a relationship because that tells me its future. Entering marriage only serves to intensify what is already present in courtship. It changes nothing. That's what was happening with Dave and

Pam. Had they gone ahead and gotten married, they would have just carried the control issue right along with them.

It doesn't take a trained professional to predict the future. Anyone can do it. All you have to do is be willing to take an honest look at the present tense of your relationship. But that seems to be a lot to ask for some couples.

I admit that honestly looking at the present tense of your relationship is not the easiest thing to do. Being truthful with yourself is an art—a skill you have to develop. It doesn't come easily, and if it comes at all, it begins when you accept the fact that *without intent and effort to change, things usually continue to be as they are.* Unless you accept that what *is* will *be,* you are not likely to give up the forms of denial that make avoiding reality such a comfortable thing to do.

If you really want to be honest concerning your relationship, ask yourself two questions: *What is really going on now?* and *For good or for bad, how is this situation affecting my relationship?* The patterns the two of you have developed are either working to (1) *enhance* your relationship (hold you and your boyfriend together and allow your relationship to grow) or to (2) *diminish* your relationship (block togetherness and push the two of you apart). Use these two terms—*enhance* and *diminish*—as guides to assess how your relationship measures up. It shouldn't be too difficult to figure out just how sound things are in your present tense and to predict exactly how sound things will be in your future.

4

Some People Aren't Marriage Material

To: Paige@College.com
From: Dad@HarveyHome.com
Subject: "First best"

Dear Paige,

Deciding to stop seeing John is one of the wisest things I have ever seen you do. I didn't have strong feelings about John, either good or bad, until I watched the two of you together this past week. That was really scary. I wondered how long it would take for you to reach the conclusion that enough was enough. Obviously, it didn't take too long.

The two of you were clearly not good for each other. But the problem was more than your simply not being a good match. As a contrast, do you remember when you and Brad broke up? It was over your "differences." Each of you really had a lot to offer

To: Paige@College.com
From: Dad@HarveyHome.com
Subject: "First best"

a relationship. You were both genuine and very willing to sacrifice for each other. But you had different dreams and wanted very different things out of life. You also needed very different things from each other. The differences between the two of you were so great that the likelihood that you could have ever fit well together was very slim. You just were not compatible.

Compatibility deals with the ease in which two people make adjustments to each other. But it operates from the assumption that at the very least, both people have something to offer a relationship. Though you and Brad did not have this ease—you didn't do well together—each of you was very capable of being in a relationship with someone else. You only needed to find a person who shared more of your dreams.

That's *not* the way it was with you and John. Your problem wasn't with differences— though you certainly had your share. It's something much more basic than that. John

To: Paige@College.com
From: Dad@HarveyHome.com
Subject: "First best"

simply has very little to offer a relationship—any relationship. He can take, but he cannot give—a fact he demonstrated repeatedly all week.

John has no respect for others. He made derogatory remarks about anyone who was overweight or underweight or of another ethnic heritage. This lack of respect for others shows itself toward you in his intense selfishness. If something is good for John, then he might do it. But if it's only good for you, then forget it. John wouldn't even do the little things you asked of him. It was obvious that his "qualities" had worn on you by the end of the week.

John's difficulty is not an issue of compatibility—it's *marriageability*. He's not suitable for a relationship with anyone regardless of who she is. John's only hope for the future rests with his ability to change some things about himself. Right now he simply has very little to give to a serious relationship, much less something as demanding as marriage.

To: Paige@College.com
From: Dad@HarveyHome.com
Subject: "First best"

Dating John, even though only for a brief time, may have been a good experience for you. Now you see more clearly what will not work in a relationship. Paige, you are a person of value and worth. God has great plans for your life. You deserve someone who will treat you right the first time, not just the second, or third, or fourth time. There is someone out there like that for you. God's design is always for the "first best" in your life. Don't ever settle for anything less.

All my love,

Dad

WHAT ARE YOU BRINGING TO YOUR RELATIONSHIP?

Whenever you are making a serious lovedecision, you have to consider what both you and your potential partner are bringing to the relationship. What are your differences? What are your similarities? How do your values line up? Are there quirks in your personalities? How have your family backgrounds and experiences shaped your lives? How do they differ? And what kind of adjustments will be called for if the two of you are going to make your marriage work?

All these questions, which address what you are bringing to the marriage, deal with compatibility. How well do you fit together? The primary assumption with compatibility is that each of you has the wherewithal to make it in some kind of relationship. So the question is whether this is the right relationship. Is he the right guy for you? Are you the right girl for him? And how easy will it be for you to make any necessary adjustments?

It's important to ask the compatibility question: *Can I make the necessary adjustments to* this *relationship?* But there's another question even more important to ask. It also has to do with what you are bringing to a marriage. But rather than dealing with compatibility, this question deals with marriageability: *Can I make the necessary adjustments to* any *relationship?* Compatibility looks at what you bring to a marriage and asks, *Can I fit with this specific person?* In contrast, marriageability looks at what you bring to a marriage and asks, *Can I fit with anyone at all?*

"WE'RE JUST DIFFERENT, THAT'S ALL"

To state it simply, some guys just aren't good marriage material. In fact, some guys have pretty deviant behavior. There's no secret about what it takes to have a good marriage. Commitment, prioritization, mutuality, respect—these are some of the essentials. But some guys don't have these baseline qualities. And having little to offer doesn't seem to slow them down too much, either.

Of course, sometimes I hear the "we're just different" excuse. You know how that works: You think exclusivity ought to be part of a committed relationship, but he sees nothing wrong with slipping around and seeing other women. When you protest, he says you're just being "too possessive." Or you think you both ought to be gainfully employed, but he's OK with your working and his hanging out with his friends. In this situation, he says you're just being "too anal." And what happens when you do press him about your complaints? Now you're being a nag, and he says, "We're just different, that's all."

No question about it, you and your boyfriend *will* have some differences. You're going to disagree on what's the best food. You're going to be a morning person, and he's going to like late nights. You may even have some differences that are so great your compatibility comes into question—like when you have significantly different views about God. But these are normal problems. They may create difficulties for you—like where you decide to eat or how you're going to worship—but they do not fall in the category of inappropriate conduct. There's not necessarily a right or wrong to them. And it is this appropriateness quality that distinguishes *different* behavior from *deviant* behavior. There is *never* an appropriate rationale for deviant behavior.

SO WHEN IS SOMETHING DEVIANT?

None of us is perfect. We all have chinks in our armor. So how do you recognize when your boyfriend has crossed the line from just being a little quirky to having a true personal problem— something that will create a problem for any relationship regardless of whom he's matched up with?

It's not always easy to distinguish between being different and being deviant. But there are some themes that can help. Obviously, if your boyfriend is doing anything either illegal or immoral, that should be a no-brainer. But when behavior is neither illegal nor blatantly immoral, how do you label it deviant? Usually I identify deviant behavior as being either *extreme* or *pervasive*—something that, unless changed, will significantly limit your relationship.

I use *extreme* as an indicator because sometimes being "excessive" is all that distinguishes something from being either normal or abnormal. I spoke with a girl who questioned whether she was marriage material because there were times when she felt "depressed." It turned out that what she labeled as depression was only occasionally feeling a little blue. She was probably describing the way we all feel. So this was neither extreme nor a real concern. I use the word *pervasive* in order to identify "frequency." Is a behavior an incident—or is it a pattern? With the exception of a few extremely inappropriate behaviors, I don't get too concerned with an occasional incident or two—an occasional harsh word or an occasional insensitivity. Sure, it would be better if your boyfriend never uttered anything but encouraging words, but that's just not reality. Even the most easygoing person will have an occasional bad day. It's when these incidents become more and more frequent—when they become patterns—that they move into the realm of deviant behavior.

The following criteria meet my definition of extreme and pervasive. Anything found in this list should prompt a red flag:

[ ] gross immaturity	[ ] unexplained changes in
[ ] emotional overreactivity	mood
[ ] highly unpredicatable	[ ] addiction (of any kind)
behavior	[ ] attempts to humiliate you
[ ] depression	[ ] attempts to devalue you

[ ] unreliability

[ ] demanding behavior

[ ] controlling behavior

[ ] untrustworthiness

[ ] pervasively self-focused

[ ] selfish

[ ] manipulative behavior

[ ] use of physical force or abuse

[ ] bizarre thoughts or behaviors

This isn't an exhaustive list, but it does give you an idea of the types of things that will significantly limit your relationship. Compatibility issues are difficult enough to adjust to. But if the guy you're interested in has a marriageability problem, there's no amount of adjustment on your part that will make a marriage work.

"FLEE, FLEE! RUN AWAY, RUN AWAY!"

What do you do if someone you care about very deeply has a significant personal problem? To quote one of the Monty Python movies, "Flee, flee! Run away, run away!" Well, maybe that's not exactly what you should do—but it's close!

The underlying principle regarding any question about emotional well-being is this: *Get it straight first!* If your boyfriend has a significant personal problem, he has little or nothing to offer to any relationship. I'm not suggesting if he's not marriage material *at this particular time* that he will not be marriage material *for all time.* Sometimes it's an issue of readiness. People can change. This change may come with maturity and the mere passage of time. It may come through therapy. God may miraculously intervene. But it must come! *Get it straight first* simply means whatever the problem, it must be dealt with and satisfactorily resolved *before* entering the relationship. Otherwise, you're just setting yourself up for disaster.

I recently saw a marriage called off because things just could not get straight. Sarah had had some concerns about her fiancé's behavior for quite some time. But she kept thinking things would change. The closer the wedding came, however, the more anxious she became. When Sarah confided in friends, they thought she was just having pre-wedding jitters. They had never seen Mike act the way Sarah described. So they advised her to go ahead with the wedding. What was Sarah to do?

"The pressure to marry was tremendous. We had sent out announcements, paid for the honeymoon, even rented an apartment," she said. And the fact that Mike was loved by Sarah's parents only served to further complicate her situation. But though surrounded by complications, Sarah chose wisdom over appeasement. Here's how she described what happened:

> It was difficult for me to call it off. The last thing I wanted to do was to hurt Mike. I really cared for him, and in his own way, I believe he cared for me, too. But he had some real problems. And I knew if things did not change in the way he treated me, it would only be a matter of time before my feelings toward him would change. We either had to get it fixed before we got married—or not get married at all. So I called it off.

Sarah had another choice. She could have postponed the wedding and offered Mike an opportunity to deal with his personal problems. That would have met the get-it-straight-first principle. But apparently Sarah was not interested in a postponement. She had seen enough. So, faced with the prospects of now or never, Sarah chose never and ended her relationship. And as she later told me, "I have no regrets."

To: Paige@College.com
From: Dad@HarveyHome.com
Subject: Time and balance

Dear Paige,

I'm glad to hear that you and Greg are finally making some "connections" (whatever that means), even though things may be moving at a slow pace. Actually, I kinda like the idea of things moving slowly. Greg sounds like a good guy. From what you tell me, he's got a lot of the values and characteristics you have grown to want and expect in someone you date. But there's nothing better than time when it comes to really getting to know someone. And it seems that time is what you are both willing to give this relationship.

Probably the thing that impresses me most about our recent conversations is the balance I'm hearing in your words. You're not just talking about the new guy in your

To: Paige@College.com
From: Dad@HarveyHome.com
Subject: Time and balance

life, not that Greg isn't important. But I'm hearing about the other important things that are happening, too—how God is dealing with your life, your embracing the responsibilities of student leadership, the ups and downs of being the editor of the school paper, the whole classroom thing, and the deepening relationships you are developing with your friends. All of these areas are important. And what's impressive is that you are allowing them to remain important in spite of Greg. That speaks to both your balance and maturity.

There is a willingness on your part to take things at a slow and easy pace with Greg. That's good. Rather than being swept away with the passion of the moment (obsessing about Greg and constantly thinking about what might be) you are content to just be (to allow the relationship to either develop or not). I see wisdom overriding the feelings of urgency. Hmmm. I guess you're growing up on me.

Your biggest fan,
Dad

"WE WENT FROM ZERO TO LOVE
IN NOTHIN' FLAT . . ."

I recently had one of those incidents on the campus of the university where I teach that literally caused me to laugh and cry at the same time. A student asked me what I thought of "quick relationships." His definition of quick was ten weeks. He had met his fiancée two months earlier. After only a few dates, they knew it was true love. Their wedding was now planned to take place in only three months.

This was the first time I had met either of them. But even though I didn't know anything about their family backgrounds or their maturity levels or even their spiritual development, I knew enough to tell them what I thought about ten-week relationships: "I think ten weeks is a good start. You certainly know each other better now than you did when you first met. But if you think you can make this kind of decision after only ten weeks, you're making a big mistake."

Neither of them looked surprised at what I had to say. I think they expected as much. I don't think they were nearly as interested in hearing my opinion as they were in telling me theirs. So they began to give me a list of reasons why their getting married was really a good idea. I listened politely for a few minutes, but then I just had to interrupt their story.

"You know, you both seem nice enough," I said. "And I'm sure that the feelings you have for each other are sincere. But no matter what you may think of each other right now, there are no princes and there are no maidens. And you haven't known each other long enough to figure that out yet.

"What's the hurry?" I asked them. "Being passionate about

one another is a good start. But it's only that—a start. It isn't love. I don't care what kind of rationales you can come up with; there's no good reason to get married quickly."

The conversation kind of dried up after that. I'm not sure what they decided to do. But it does concern me that they might have actually followed through with their plans.

There was nothing wrong with where they were in their relationship. Every relationship starts somewhere. The problem was with where they *thought* they were. They reminded me of the words from a country song: "We went from zero to love in nothin' flat." Those words may make fine lyrics for a song, but they miss reality by a bunch. You can move from zero to passion that quickly, but not from zero to love. My young couple had what *felt* like love. But *real* love takes a lot longer to develop.

EARLY LOVE

When I think of quick relationships, I am reminded of the story Jesus told about the sower (see Matthew 13:3–8). When the sower cast out his seed, it landed on four different types of soil. Some seed fell on the footpath. This soil was so hard, the seed could not even take root. The birds ate it. Some fell on rocky soil, where it was able to take root and quickly grow into plants. That sounds OK—and the plants even looked great for a while. But then the sun began to beat down on them. Because the roots could not grow deeply into the ground, the plants could not draw moisture, and they soon "withered away." Some seed fell among the thistles. Though these seeds were able to sprout, the thistles soon choked them out. Finally, some seed fell on good soil. According to the parable, it was only this seed that was able to root, grow strong, and bear much fruit.

I could compare the plants that sprang up from these four different types of soil to various relationships. But the most striking comparison to quick relationships is found with those plants growing in the rocky soil. These plants looked good. But because they had no depth, they were very unstable. The heat from the sun easily beat them down. That's the way it is with relationships during early love. These relationships look good, and they feel even better. But they have no depth. They have no depth because depth is something that only comes with time. Their basic instability makes it difficult for early love relationships to withstand outside pressures.

TWO FORMULAS FOR SUCCESS

A colleague of mine stated the principle best when he said, "Couples need to experience every season together." Really getting to know someone is a complicated process, and there are no shortcuts. So part of experiencing every season involves doing the *time* it takes to really get to know each other. Research suggests that two years is a good minimum. So if you really want to increase your chances of having a successful marriage, follow one of these formulas:

> Short courtship + long engagement = two years
> Long courtship + short engagement = two years

I guess there could be other variations of these formulas, like equal lengths of both courtship and engagement. But you get the idea. The underlying principle is this: It takes time to really get to know someone well enough to marry him.

I like to push the idea of *seasons* past the point where it simply includes the passage of time. I think a calendar is important or I wouldn't be talking about two years being a minimum length of time for courtship and engagement. But you can also measure seasons by the *experiences* you share together.

It has been said that you do not really know a person well enough to marry him until you have sweated, pondered, grunted, tried, failed, and succeeded with him. That seems to cover a lot of territory. We need to get past the point where we're just "putting our best foot forward." I remember a couple telling me they thought they were making headway in their relationship because they had experienced and survived their first argument. There was some truth in what they had to say. Decisions to marry need to be made resolutely. And resolute decisions are based on knowledge of, not ignorance about, one another. This kind of knowledge only comes through experiencing life together.

THE TEFLON MENTALITY

If you cooked the way I do, you too would view the nonstick surfaces on pots and pans as one of the great technical advances of the modern age. No matter what you do—sautéing, deep-frying, pan-searing—nothing sticks to them. These pans have saved my bacon several times. Actually, what Teflon has allowed me to do is to successfully avoid the consequences of my behavior. Rather than experiencing the result of using too much heat (I'm not a patient cook) and maybe learning from my mistakes the truth that slower is usually better, this technology has allowed countless meals to escape being stuck permanently to the bottom of my pans.

Teflon may work well on pots and pans, but it doesn't translate well to other areas of our lives. I have met many Christians who have converted Teflon from a product that covers pots and pans to an attitude about life. They have what I call a Teflon mentality. You embrace a Teflon mentality when you believe the rules that apply to other people do not apply to you because you are a Christian (and therefore special). As one newly engaged young woman phrased it, "It's OK for us to marry [though they had dated for only six months] because of the God thing." By "the God thing," she was referring to the fact that she and her fiancé were both Christians so they were automatically exempted from the normal rules of courtship.

This idea of exemption was pushed to an extreme by one of my graduate students. He wasn't married, and though he posed this as a serious question, I think he may have been making a feeble attempt at humor. He asked, "Just how much credit do I get in your formula for marital success by being a Christian? Is it worth six months of dating? Could it even equal a year?"

I think he was joking. But not taking any chances, I told him that he got no credit at all. And as one of his classmates was quick to point out, being Christian can even have its downside. "It's unrealistic to think that, just because you're both Christians, you're going to totally see eye to eye on everything," she said. "Some of our [referring to her own fiancé] biggest fights have been over religion!"

God grants no exemptions. Scripture teaches patience—not impulsivity (see Galatians 5:22). We are to pray for wisdom, not to act on passion alone. There is no right reason to do the wrong thing, and hurrying to marriage, for whatever reason, is wrong. Slow down and let the relationship happen. It only makes good sense.

6

Everybody Brings Something to Marriage

To: Paige@College.com
From: Dad@HarveyHome.com
Subject: Good question

Dear Paige,

I'm glad you took the time to tell me about Tim, the new guy in your life. From your description, he sounds really nice—you know, the part about his being bright, a committed Christian, and seeming to genuinely care about your feelings. Just so you'll know, those are the kinds of things dads like to see in the men who date their daughters. If he hangs around long enough, maybe I'll get a chance to meet him. (That's a little "dad humor.")

Though Tim and I haven't met yet, I still want to make a couple of observations based on some things you have said about him. You said he confused you with his "guarded behavior." He's a good listener but

To: Paige@College.com
From: Dad@HarveyHome.com
Subject: Good question

isn't really much of a talker, at least when it comes to sharing a lot of personal stuff about himself. Your question was, "Why would he be so guarded when I haven't given him any reason not to trust me?"

That's a good question, and I'm impressed that you even noticed something like that. Usually we're so caught up in the moment that we overlook some of the little things that really aren't so little. But about your confusion, my best guess is that Tim's tendency to guard his feelings has a whole lot more to do with him than it does with you—and also a lot more to do with what has gone on in the past than in the present. That doesn't make it unimportant. But it does make it a little more understandable.

You and Tim are both bringing some "less than obvious" things to this relationship. That's true with anyone. You both have pasts and have been influenced by these different experiences. This is especially true of family influences. The things that attract

To: Paige@College.com
From: Dad@HarveyHome.com
Subject: Good question

you to Tim—his interest in spiritual things, his willingness to accept a challenge, his genuine interest in you—these are probably all true. But they are the most visible. They are the "here and now." What's harder to see is where these things come from and what else may be lurking just a little deeper.

If Tim is guarded, it's probably something he learned at home. Home might not have been a real safe place—at least when it came to sharing his feelings. Maybe no one really had the time—or the interest—to listen. That's not the way it was for you, Paige. We encouraged you to talk and tried to provide an environment of acceptance. I think you felt free to share at home, and you continue to feel free in other relationships. Maybe it's difficult to understand why Tim finds this hard to do when you find it so easy. In that we still have a tremendous long-distance phone bill, maybe we did too good a job (a little more dad humor).

Paige, I am proud of the person you are

To: Paige@College.com
From: Dad@HarveyHome.com
Subject: Good question

becoming. You seem to learn something new from each relationship you're in. Learning's good—though not always comfortable. So as you continue to make those lovedecisions, remember this: No matter how things look in the present, when you marry someone, you'll also marry his past—and he will marry yours. There's always more there than easily meets the eye, and that stuff won't just go away. You're each bringing a lot to the mix. So you'll need to look deeply before going forward.

Ever thankful for your growing insight,

Dad

PETER AND KATIE

"Things are going to have to change, or I don't know if I can stay in this marriage." That was one of Peter's opening lines in our first therapy session. As the session continued, he even tossed around the D word. Now, I'm a marriage therapist, and it's not real uncommon for me to hear couples talk about divorce. What concerned me about

Peter and Katie was that they had only been married a year, and this kind of talk was coming up. How did things get so desperate so fast?

You wouldn't think by looking at Peter and Katie that they'd be likely candidates to end up in a therapist's office. On the surface, they seemed to have a lot of things going for them—the kinds of things we professionals look for as potential indicators of success in relationships. They came from intact and strongly religious homes, and they shared many of the same values; plus, each professed strong religious convictions. They spoke of loving each other and of having a commitment to being married. And though they were young (college aged), they were not *too* young. Katie, who had only recently finished college, had already started her career. And though Peter had not yet completed his college degree, he was in school and seemed to know what he wanted to do with his life. So far, so good. So where was the problem?

Peter and Katie had known each other for three years prior to getting married. That seemed long enough for two people in the lovedecisions stage of life to make an intelligent decision. But there was a possible glitch in this time frame—the kind of glitch that plays havoc with my "formulas for success." Much of their three years had been spent as a long-distance relationship with them actually having little face-to-face contact. They had reasoned that their quality time together easily made up for the lack of quantity time. As they sat in my office for their initial therapy session, they were both beginning to rethink that idea.

Initially, Peter did most of the serious talking and with statements like, "Maybe we're just not right for each other" and "I wonder if we've gone too far to get what we had back" and "I've been surprised with some of the new things I've learned about

Katie this year," he made it pretty clear where he stood. He said he was "fed up" and "close to calling it quits."

But where was Katie in this relationship? Was she as miserable as Peter? And even if she was, was she as ready to throw in the towel? I seemed to be gathering a lot of "Katie questions" when she decided to speak up and give me her thoughts.

If being fed up was Peter's theme, confusion was Katie's. She didn't have a clue about what was going on with Peter. "I thought I knew him pretty well, but this isn't the man I married." The best she could figure out was that Peter didn't like her "directness." If she said anything with even a hint of disapproval, Peter defined it as her being upset and their having an argument, and took those signals as his cue to walk out.

So this was the situation: Two people who appeared to have everything going for them were finding that just maybe some things might have been overlooked. And now, in utter confusion, they were both asking the question, "Who is this person I have married?" It made me wonder what they had seen in each other in the first place.

FIRST ATTRACTERS

"What first attracted you to Katie?" I asked Peter. He hesitated for a moment. I don't think he was ready for that kind of question. After all, he was here to list his grievances, not to talk about Katie's good points. Still, Peter mustered up a response. Of course, he found Katie attractive—and they did share a lot in common. But he was really attracted to her independent spirit. "She knew what she wanted in life and wasn't afraid to go after it," Peter said.

I asked Katie the same question. Unlike Peter, Katie didn't

hesitate before responding: "At first it was because I thought he was good-looking. But what kept me interested was his *ease.* He was just so gentle, so easy to be with." Katie went on to say their similar values and goals in life had been another attracter, though she added, "I'm not so sure that's the case anymore. Maybe that's part of our problem."

THE ICEBERG MENTALITY

As Peter and Katie continued to talk about their dating years, what struck me most was just how much they had operated from an iceberg mentality. I'm sure you're familiar with the structure of icebergs. Though they appear to be floating on the surface of the water, only 10 percent of the iceberg is actually visible. Most of the massive structure is out of view. Well, people are a whole lot like icebergs. Peter and Katie saw the superficial characteristics easily enough—the stuff floating on top. But neither of them really looked much below the surface to see what lurked beneath the water line.

Maybe if they had spent some "real time" together during their three-year courtship—had they worked together, sweat together, cried together, fought together, etc.—some of what was really there might have surfaced. (That's the problem with couples' long-distance relationships. They tend to put their best foot forward when they're together. After all, why should they spend the little time they have together arguing? Instead they put aside their differences and just enjoy being with each other.) But there was no guarantee that spending more time together would have gotten them past the superficial aspects of their relationship. Many of us in "real courtships" still fail to see beneath the surface. For one reason or another, we miss what's really there. So what had Peter and Katie missed?

WHAT THEY FAILED TO SEE

What Peter and Katie saw in each other was true enough. Peter did have an easygoing nature, and Katie was independent. But what they failed to see were where these tendencies came from and just how complexly they were tied to other things. For certain, there are a lot of things that help make up the unseen portion of your personal iceberg. But there is nothing that more consistently influences who you are than your family. That was the case with Peter and Katie. They both had failed to see that they were extensions of their families. And as extensions, each naturally brought some "baggage" to their relationship. It was this baggage that kept getting in the way of their having a rewarding marriage.

Peter came from a very close-knit family. Both his parents were soft spoken, and he described his father as being easygoing and godly and his mother as a "Martha Stewart lookalike." He never saw them argue and couldn't remember so much as a cross word that had passed between them. Peter was the only son with three sisters, two older and one younger. Perfect stairsteps in birth, the children were separated by about a year. Peter was especially close to his two older sisters, who seemed to compete with Mom for the privilege of taking care of him. The only tension he remembered came from conflict between his oldest and youngest sisters. When they went head to head, he just left the room and got out of the line of fire. "I couldn't stand to be around the fussing."

Katie's family was less ideal. Though there was no question

that her parents loved each other, their relationship was tension filled. This was largely due to her father's tendency to be stubborn and insensitive. He never really attempted to meet his wife's needs though he fully expected her to meet his. Katie's mother tried to measure up but could never do enough. And there were some sacrifices she was just unwilling to make. Over the years, the tension overwhelmed Katie's mother and gradually wore her down emotionally. Watching all of this had an effect on Katie. She become angry at her father's insensitivity and her mother's willingness to allow it.

Katie also had three siblings, but unlike Peter, she was the oldest. This put a lot of responsibility on her as she frequently helped her mother take care of the younger children. Responsibility was not foreign to Katie because circumstances in her life had been more difficult for her than for Peter. But this only made her more determined. Her success in life—and she *was* successful—had come as a result of her willingness to work hard and to face head-on any hardship that came her way.

These are only thumbnail sketches of Peter and Katie's family lives. But even these brief glimpses "below the water line" helped to make sense of their situation. Peter was easygoing, all right. And as long as Katie was content to just take care of things (as his mother and sisters had done), everything was fine. But the moment Katie became displeased with Peter's easygoing nature—when she viewed him as maybe *too* easygoing—and began to put pressure on him to "change," everything began to break down. Remember, Peter does not like conflict. And he learned that when conflict enters the picture, it's time for him to leave. As he said in our session, "I just don't understand why things can't be easier than this."

Peter's attraction to Katie's independent qualities also began to make more sense. Katie's willingness to take care of things (as Peter's sisters had done) meant there was less for him to have to do. What he failed to see was that Katie believed he ought to also pitch in. She thought that he too needed to be responsible. But she also thought he ought to seize the moment—to take charge. Remember, Katie had accomplished a lot in her life because she had been willing to work through any hardship. She believed in sacrifice. Peter had a different set of guidelines when it came to what constituted sacrifice; when the going got tough, he punted. This difference explained why Peter was still in school working on a degree while Katie had already finished and had begun her career. Was that bad? Not necessarily. But it *was* different.

The longer Peter and Katie were together, the more apparent their differences became. When Katie tried to talk to Peter about her concerns, it felt like conflict to him, and he did what he had always done: He fled the scene. This frustrated Katie because it struck a very old nerve. She had seen this type of insensitivity in her parents' marriage. Katie hadn't liked it in theirs, and she sure didn't like it in her own. But unlike her mother, she wasn't willing to tolerate it. So she pressed even harder for Peter to "stay in the game"—to deal with her complaints. And the cycle began. It didn't take long for this pattern to completely cripple their marriage.

EVERYBODY BRINGS SOMETHING

As we got toward the end of the session, I commented to Peter and Katie, "You both sure have brought a lot of home into your marriage." They looked surprised. They still weren't getting it. Katie didn't say anything, in part because she didn't know how Peter might take it. But Peter had a different assessment. "All we need to do is to learn how to communicate better." He wanted me to give them a book to read and some communication exercises to practice. That would fix what was wrong. In a way, Peter was correct. He and Katie did need to learn to communicate better. But this learning wasn't going to come by simply reading a book. They both needed to learn a lot more about themselves—and about each other. They needed to get below the water line. And if they could get the big picture, they would then need to take responsibility for what they found.

KNOW YOUR STUFF

When I speak to groups in the lovedecisions phase of life, what I have to say always focuses on one of two topics. I either talk about the prerequisites to moving into the next phase of life (marriage) or the characteristics of a healthy relationship. If you look at the way this book is laid out, you'll see that's what's in it. Well, one of the big prerequisites to moving to the next level—at least, if you're going to make a successful jump—is knowing your stuff. And by *stuff* I mean knowing what you're bringing into the marriage and knowing what your boyfriend's bringing too.

Everybody has stuff. You can't ignore the past. No matter how good things look in the present (on the surface), there has always been a past. Examining your past isn't necessarily about contrasting good with bad. It may be that you're only discovering your differences. We've all had influences that have helped in a very positive way to bring us to where we are today. But even differences require adjustments. For that reason alone you need to look beneath the surface and ask, "What am I bringing to this relationship?" and "What are you bringing?" Remember, everybody brings something.

PART 2

SIX QUESTIONS YOU NEED TO ASK ABOUT YOUR RELATIONSHIP

7

Are Things Getting Better—for Me and for Us?

To: Paige@College.com
From: Dad@HarveyHome.com
Subject: Healthy redecorating

Dear Paige,

I chuckled after hanging up the phone last night. Some of the things you said about your breakup with Brad kept going through my mind. Things like your doing some "healthy redecorating" in your room and your need to create a "Brad-free" environment. Those thoughts kept colliding with some other mental images I was having of your making a clean sweep of pictures and keepsakes—I guess that's one way to get a clean dorm room.

Chuckles weren't the only feelings. There was also a sense of relief. I'm glad to see you guys break up. Don't get me wrong. I liked Brad OK. I still do. He's a good guy. I just think he'll be better with someone else.

To: Paige@College.com
From: Dad@HarveyHome.com
Subject: Healthy redecorating

You and Brad just didn't seem to be good for each other. When you were together, you were either up or down—and mostly down. You always seemed to be crying. And like you said last night, you never want to cry that much in a relationship again.

I know you cared a lot for Brad. And from all I could tell, he cared a lot for you, too. In some ways, maybe you guys did love each other. But real love makes you a better person—and I never saw that happening when the two of you were together. I think you each needed something from the other that neither of you could give. Brad seemed to need you to be more of a follower—to be more dependent on him and to allow him to lead. You needed him be more flexible— to allow you to be more of your own person. Because you had such different needs, your relationship never got easy. You were both always on your guard.

Paige, you are about the most caring person I know. There's a kindness about you

To: Paige@College.com
From: Dad@HarveyHome.com
Subject: Healthy redecorating

that could only have come from your mother. But you also have your sensitive spots. Brad knew where every one of your hot buttons was located, and he got real good at punching them. Your arguing became a recurring theme. It wasn't a good sign that you argued as much as you did at the beginning of your relationship. But an even worse sign was that your arguing didn't improve over time.

I want you to have someone in your life who brings out the best in you—not the worst. That's what you deserve. I know there's someone like that out there for you. If you're not with someone who is doing that, then you're not with the right guy. So don't give up—and don't settle. You deserve only the best.

Always in your corner,

Dad

THINGS OUGHT TO BE GETTING BETTER

A man was talking to me about some concerns in his life when I asked him how things were going in his marriage. He hesitated for a second and then said, "My marriage is OK. It's not great, but I've been married seventeen years. I don't expect it to be like it was when we first got married. I mean, life gets in the way and things change."

I thought about what he said for a few minutes then responded, "You're right. Things do change between two people in a marriage. They get better." Now, of course, I know things don't always get better between two people. I'm a therapist, so I know stuff like that. But things *ought* to get better as a marriage rolls through the years!

Better—isn't that an interesting term? Think about it. You really can't define what *better* is by itself. It only makes sense when it is compared to something else. So things are either better than they were, or they are not better than they were— whatever "were" was. *Better* speaks of movement and direction and asks the question, "Where is this thing going?"

When it comes to intimate relationships, with the passage of time, things ought to get better. This movement toward better actually takes on two different meanings for you and your boyfriend. First, things ought to be better for you personally. And second, things ought to be better for the two of you together. Let's look at both of these improvements.

"IS THIS RELATIONSHIP MAKING ME A BETTER PERSON?"

Being in a relationship with your boyfriend ought to be making you a better person. Now, we can't put all the responsibility for who you are on him; that's not what I'm suggesting at all. The only person who's ultimately responsible for you is you. But being in a love relationship will influence you—for good or for bad. So is this involvement making you (influencing you to be) a better person—or not?

One day last year, I was speaking to a student who admitted her date life could be summed up under the heading "Why does loving you make me feel so bad?" During the time she had been dating her boyfriend, her confidence in her own ability to make decisions had decreased, she had gone from feeling cheerful and carefree to sad and constricted, and from being outgoing and social to withdrawn and closed off. To top it off, she had steadily developed a long list of physical ailments. She began our talk by saying, "I feel as bad about myself as I have ever felt in my entire life!"

It seemed a good time for me to ask exactly where she thought this relationship was taking her. "If things don't change in the way Mark is treating me, and if I stay with him, my headaches will increase, and I will continue to fall apart—both emotionally and physically. If I break it off, I will become a better person." She had figured out the direction this relationship was heading, she had figured out the cause, and a little while later, she figured out the solution. She dumped Mark.

"WHAT MAKES ME BETTER?"

There's no secret to at least one of the factors that make us better people. It has to do with whom we let into our lives. Old and New Testament scriptures alike warn us of the influence our "associates" have on our lives (see, for example, 1 Kings 11:2 and James 4:4). And we're fooling ourselves if we think that somehow this doesn't apply to each of us. None of us is beyond influence. So we're to put ourselves in relationships with people who are good for us—and not toxic. We place people in our lives who take seriously Paul's directive that we are to "build one another up" instead of tearing each other down (1 Thessalonians 5:11).

I use the term *esteeming* to summarize Paul's thoughts on building up and tearing down. We are to esteem and to be esteemed. So the question for you to ask yourself now becomes, "Am I being esteemed in my relationship?" There are lots of things that go into esteeming the one you love. But let's look at what your boyfriend says and does as a quick reference point. Does your boyfriend say the kinds of things that make you feel like he believes in you—the kinds of things that build your self-esteem? Or does he say things that put you down? Does your boyfriend do the kinds of things that make you feel valued and special? Do you feel cared for? Or does he do things that embarrass you—that cause you to feel small in his eyes and in the eyes of your friends? As a result of being in this relationship, do you feel more confident? Do you feel more competent? Has your self-worth grown? Do you feel more at ease? Are you becoming more spiritual? What he says and does is either building you up or tearing you down, and—surprise!—only one of those will make you a better person.

I am a better person because of Jan—because of her love, her assurance, her support. And she is a better person because of me. That's the way it is supposed to be. In the things we say and do, and in our attitudes, we esteem one another. You deserve to be in a relationship with someone who esteems you, too—someone who will only bring out the best in you.

"IS THIS RELATIONSHIP GETTING BETTER?"

My theme of movement and change—that things ought to be getting better—is not only true for you as a person but also for your relationship. What's going on between the two of you— your communication, understanding, etc.—ought to be continually growing in a positive way. But what exactly does *better* look like when it comes to a relationship? Christian marital therapist and prolific author H. Norman Wright helps shed light on this by likening a couple's engagement to the "fruit of the Spirit" described in Galatians 5:22. He has developed a set of questions based on this spiritual theme that assesses exactly where an engagement is heading. I have included his questions so you can do some checking on your own.

ASSESSING THE DIRECTION OF ENGAGEMENT

1. The fruit of the Spirit is love:
   Is there an increasing concern for each other in your engagement?

   Yes   No

2. The fruit of the Spirit is joy:
   Is there an increasing season of gladness in your engagement?

   Yes   No

3. The fruit of the Spirit is peace:
   Is there an increased quiet in your hearts, in your love?

   Yes   No

---

4. The fruit of the Spirit is long-suffering:
   Is there an increasing stretch in your attitudes?

   Yes   No

5. The fruit of the Spirit is gentleness:
   Are you increasingly kind, more courteous, softer in your touch?

   Yes   No

6. The fruit of the Spirit is meekness:
   Is there a growing self-honesty in each of you?

   Yes   No

7. The fruit of the Spirit is goodness:
   More and more, do you seek to be a blessing?

   Yes   No

8. The fruit of the Spirit is faith:
   Are your fears on the decline?

   Yes   No

9. The fruit of the Spirit is temperance:
   Are you more and more in charge of your emotions?

   Yes   No

The sense of movement is illustrated in Dr. Wright's use of words such as *increasingly, growing,* and *blessing.* He is asking, "Are things getting better in these ways?" You should be able to answer yes to each of these questions. If not, then you have to ask, "Why not?"

I like the way Dr. Wright gets to the heart of the matter with very specific questions. But when I'm speaking to people in the lovedecisions phase, I usually try to get to the heart of the matter by asking one simple question: "Is it getting easier?"

This tells me all I need to know.

IS IT GETTING EASIER?

I was talking with a young friend recently just before he got married. He was filling me in on all the details of the wedding-planning process. Deep down, he was ready to get past all the frenzy that went with "getting" married to actually "living" married life. We were about halfway through our conversation when he made a directional statement. "You know, it's like you said it would be," he told me. "Things have just gotten so much easier between us."

Matt wasn't referring to the flurry of activities surrounding Melanie and him. It was currently anything but calm. After all, they were planning a wedding, looking at job changes, and wrestling with having to move. But what was going on between them—how they related to each other in the midst of the turmoil—was "easier."

Now, we all have our moments. Even the best relationships have times of tension—when our nerves get frayed and we say things we shouldn't say. But the important question is, How are you and your boyfriend relating? Are things getting easier—or are they getting more difficult?

Some old marital sayings have stuck with me over the years.

I remember Jan's grandmother saying, "You don't spit on me; I won't spit on you." I'm not sure there's scriptural support for this principle of life, but it's always made sense to me. One saying with a little more application to what we're talking about here came from a close friend. She said, "Don't marry anyone you'll have to drag through life." She was speaking from experience, having dragged someone through many years of (married) life. What she didn't know when she made this statement was that she was really saying, *Don't marry anyone if the relationship isn't getting easier.* From the start of her relationship, she had been the one doing all the emotional work. She held on to the dream that things would change, that surely things would improve. They didn't for her—and they probably won't for you.

WHAT DOES "GETTING EASIER" LOOK LIKE?

Getting easier involves more stuff than I can easily list. But some of the conditions suggesting that you're moving in the right direction would include:

- Finding more and more things you agree on
versus more and more things you disagree on.

- Discovering an increasing ability to resolve issues between you—to sign off on the deal—
versus feeling like you haven't been heard or you're just "agreeing to disagree."

- Finding a positive change in the way you talk to each other—more personal and direct—
versus having to stick to superficial subjects or "walk on eggshells."

- Experiencing a growing sense of comfort—support, acceptance, and caring—
  versus feeling anxious and wondering if you can ever measure up or do enough.

- Having a growing sense of trust in what he says and does versus questioning your boyfriend's words, motivations, and behavior.

THE BOTTOM LINE

Are things getting better? That's the question we started with, and it's all about direction. The long and the short of it is this: Things ought to be getting better—moving in a good direction—for you and between you. And if they aren't, it's time to take a long, hard look at what you're becoming.

8

Is Control an Issue?

To: Paige@College.com
From: Dad@HarveyHome.com
Subject: Sandy

Dear Paige,

I just wanted to follow up on your call last night about your friend Sandy. First of all, I think you are showing you're a true friend by being willing to talk to her about your concerns. A lot of people can see what's going on and even feel for their friends, but they still do nothing. They're afraid that talking might hurt their friendship, so they don't take the risk. True friends—the kind I want around me—care enough to act. That's what you've done for Sandy.

What you described last night (her boyfriend returning to town unexpectedly and flying into a rage because Sandy wasn't at her apartment when he called) is bad enough. But for him to then track her

To: Paige@College.com
From: Dad@HarveyHome.com
Subject: Sandy

down at an all-school function and demand that she leave and come with him was more than insensitive—it was controlling. Didn't he do something similar a few months ago? That's even more troubling because it means we're seeing a pattern. My guess is there have been lots of these incidents out there that you're not even aware of.

Paige, you have every right to be concerned for Sandy. Sandy should be concerned for Sandy! She is in an abusive relationship. Her recognizing that she feels upset and disappointed is a good sign. And her questioning whether marrying her boyfriend is the right thing is an even better one. There are so many red flags with this relationship that she'd have to be blind not to see them.

If Sandy isn't ready to end this relationship, she at least needs to call a time-out and take a closer look—with the help of a profes-sional. One of my fears for Sandy though is that she won't do either. Too often, people in these types of relationships just make up

To: Paige@College.com
From: Dad@HarveyHome.com
Subject: Sandy

and pretend things are going to be different. It wouldn't even surprise me if Sandy started feeling somehow responsible for her boyfriend's behavior—that she's somehow causing him to act the way he does. This is completely false!

Recognize your boundaries, Paige. You can't make Sandy's decisions for her. Nor can you control what she does. But you can keep on being a true friend. She probably needs you more now than ever before.

Well, enough about Sandy. I can't help but think about you when I think about her situation. I know you've never dated anyone who treated you like this. And I doubt that you would. I know you—and you won't be controlled. But I just want you to understand what you really do need in a relationship. You are a pretty independent person, and that's OK. But not every guy will feel comfortable with that. Just make sure that your guy does. You need a man who won't be intimidated by your independence—one

To: Paige@College.com
From: Dad@HarveyHome.com
Subject: Sandy

who won't have to have the final word, who will treat you as an equal and who will make decisions with you and not for you. That may sound like a tall order—but there's someone out there who'll fit the bill. So keep up the search.

Keep on doing what you think is best.

Dad

IT'S ALL ABOUT POWER

Control is always about power. And when it becomes a problem for a relationship, it always boils down to balance gone awry— somebody wants more than he or she ought to have. I spoke with a young lady recently who described "the straw that broke the camel's back" in her previous relationship. Apparently her boyfriend said one too many times that she "lacked Christian virtues" because she wouldn't agree with something he had said. He wasn't "into" independence—at least not in the women he dated. Another girl described a relationship in which her boyfriend edited the events of their life together. And his editing always had the same theme: "No matter what we did, he always came across as wise and superior, and I was always stupid. I began to feel so bad when I was with him." Yet another spoke of fear: "He never wanted me to be with my friends. And if I spent some time with them anyway, I never knew what kind of mood he'd be in or what he might do."

What do all these situations share in common? Each one is about control in the relationship—who has it and who doesn't. And each of these relationships was out of balance. Control is always about power. The person who wants all the power wants to control the relationship. He wants the last word in any decisions. He wants things done his way. And to get this control, he needs to be superior and you need to be inferior.

So what do you need to know about controlling relationships? Three simple facts:

1. *They're about tearing you down.* Controlling relationships are not about building you up. They're about putting you down—and keeping you there.

2. *They're based on weakness.* Control never comes from strength because a healthy person doesn't have the need to control you. Only someone with insecurities will try to do that.

3. *It takes two people to keep it going.* There are two roles played in a true power imbalance: First, there is the person who needs to be in control (who has the need to dominate). Second, there is the person who is willing (allows herself) to be controlled. If either of you stopped playing your role, the relationship would have to change.

SO, WHEN IS IT CONTROL?

Just because you have a disagreement or occasionally argue doesn't make your boyfriend a controlling person. Let's face it.

We all have times of conflict. But what are the themes and patterns that keep resurfacing in your relationship? Is disagreement even allowed? When is it control—and when is it not? Here are some clues to help you decide for yourself. It's probably control when the following situations occur repeatedly.

When everything is an issue

All relationships will have problems that arise from time to time. But when "everything" becomes an issue, something else is going on. Remember, control is about power, and a controlling boyfriend wants to have all the say. So forget about any rights you think you might have! You are expected to play by his rules—and that means no rights for you.

If you're in a relationship where everything ends up in an argument, that's probably a sign that you haven't learned the rules yet. You still think you're in an equal partnership. Want to see the arguing stop? That's simple enough. Just give in and let him have his way on everything every time. The arguing will stop, all right! But only because you've finally learned the rules and given up all of your rights. With him in charge, there isn't anything left to argue about.

When everything gets turned into a competition

"He never shares my joy," a woman in a controlling relationship might say. "If I do well at something, he just starts talking about what he's done and how what I did wasn't really all that great. I always feel so put down. Everything gets turned into some kind of competition. Can't I just be OK for once?"

Competition in a relationship is just another opportunity to figure out who's got the power. If your boyfriend can't share your joy—if he can't feel good about who you are and what you've done—then why not? This is a giant red flag.

When the best you can do is to agree to disagree

When it comes to resolving disagreements, I guess "agreeing to disagree" is better than nothing. But if that's the best you can do—ever—then you're in real trouble. Whenever there is an issue to be resolved (and if it gets resolved), there are four possible choices: After discussion, you can honestly decide (not just in resignation, but in an honest agreement) to do it his way; you can honestly decide to do it your way; you can honestly decide on a compromise between his way and your way; or you can decide to agree to disagree.

There are some situations when deciding to agree to disagree will just have to do. But the frequency with which this occurs over the other (better) options needs to be so small that it's almost negligible. If this is the way you and your boyfriend usually solve your problems, I doubt that much real resolution is taking place. It's usually an indication of a power struggle where at least one of you wants to call all the shots. So ask what is really going on because this is another huge red flag.

When you feel manipulated

"If you loved me, you'd _____(fill in the blank)." Ever heard these words? Did you feel good when you heard them—or did you feel bad? Manipulation is a subtle form of control that attempts to get you to do something you don't really want to do. It makes you feel bad because it eats away at the trust you want to place in your boyfriend. Instead of trusting that he is genuinely interested in what's best for you, you begin to sense that he's mostly interested in watching out for number one and what you ought to give up for him.

When your relationship is marked with jealousy

He says, "I don't want you even talking to any other guys!" You respond, "But I've got some guy friends—some longtime guy friends." He then makes his point clear: "I don't care—I don't want you doing it!"

Jealousy is a common characteristic of controlling boyfriends. Remember, the need to control springs from weakness, not from strength. A boyfriend who needs to control is basically insecure, so how could he trust that all you're interested in is just talking to another guy? He can't take the risk. He's got to protect what's his.

When he constantly wants to isolate you from your friends

"And you spend too much time with your friends, too," a controlling boyfriend might say. His jealousy extends beyond just other guys. It includes *all* your friends. Any time spent with them is too much! Anything that pulls you away from him is an interference. If you're beginning to feel cut off from everyone else but your boyfriend, it may be because you *are* cut off from everyone but your boyfriend. By keeping you from your friends, he increases his influence over you and your dependence on him—an intentional goal of a controlling boyfriend.

When he makes decisions for you instead of with you

This is about who really has the right to make decisions in your relationship. From the perspective of a controlling boyfriend, it is he who has the ultimate authority. Whether it occurs as "my way or no way" or "it's not a done deal until I say it's a done deal," it all turns out the same. Your boyfriend has the last word and is the ultimate decision maker because he believes that is his right.

When you can't seem to ever measure up

Can't do enough to make him happy? No matter how much you give up for your boyfriend—friends, beliefs, dreams—it's not enough? Maybe it's not you. Just maybe it's him. Some guys are rattled by even the hint of independence. Unless they have all of you—all of your time, allegiance, and obedience—they're not satisfied. In controlling relationships, measuring up comes with a pretty high price tag.

When you don't feel safe around him

Do you fear that your boyfriend might do something to physically harm you if you do something to displease him? You don't have to have been hit in order to fear him. Intimidation and the threat of physical violence can be just as controlling. But safety is even broader than physical concerns. Sometimes words can hurt as much as physical blows. So how safe do you feel?

WHEN IS IT BALANCED?

A couple who had been married a few years met with a group of my lovedecisions folks and talked about their courtship. Cindy made some interesting observations about Rob during their dating years—characteristics he had carried into their marriage. Her observations included statements such as, "He wasn't intimidated by my independence," "He didn't feel threatened and react when I had a different opinion," and "He was his own person and was free to support and encourage me."

Now, all of this sounds pretty good to me. It sounds healthy. It sounds loving. It sounds balanced. And it doesn't sound controlling. So, following their lead, what would a power-balanced relationship with your boyfriend look like? Probably something like this:

- He sees both sides of an issue instead of only his.

- Every decision doesn't become a struggle. He doesn't have to win.

- Decisions are mutual. You have a right and a vote.

- He supports you rather than puts you down.

- He shares your joy (successes) rather than discounting your accomplishments.

- He allows you your space and your friends so you can have a life apart from him.

- He treats you with respect, and you have no fear.

- You've learned to trust that he will always do what is in your best interest.

In a healthy relationship, you're a companion and not a piece of property—the way God intended.

WHAT TO DO IF YOU'RE IN
A CONTROLLING RELATIONSHIP

If you're in a controlling relationship, the important thing to know is that you don't have to stay there. Sure, it's hard to make sense of the mess you're in. You may find yourself wondering, *How did I get here in the first place?* Maybe you grew up with a controlling parent, and it didn't feel all that different from what you were used to. Maybe it started out good and just gradually turned into something bad. Maybe he's telling you it isn't bad, and you don't know whether to believe him or your own feelings. After all, it's been a long time since you trusted anything that you thought—especially if it was different from his opinions—and it's hard to start thinking for yourself again. Maybe you've just been holding on to the dream that things will change, that they will get better. And, of course, it's always easier to get into something than it is to get out of it.

It doesn't matter how you got there—or why you've stayed. All that really matters is that now you see what's happening and you know that you don't want to live this way any longer. You may need to get some help from a professional. Sure, your friends can be helpful. But they are limited. So get whatever help you need in order to get your life back. The Control Quiz, which follows, is a good place to start.

THE CONTROL QUIZ

Still confused? Maybe this will help. Answer these fifteen questions, realizing that even one yes answer means you should take a closer look at your relationship.

TOP FIFTEEN SUBTLE INDICATIONS
THAT I'M BEING CONTROLLED

1. I find myself apologizing a lot for my behavior.
    Yes   No

2. I begin to doubt the soundness of my judgment.
    Yes   No

3. I begin to feel unsure about my intellectual ability.
    Yes   No

4. My self-esteem is not as high as it used to be.
    Yes   No

5. I used to argue more with my boyfriend, but now I just give in. Why hassle? He's probably right anyway.
    Yes   No

6. I really need to make more of an effort to look nicer.
    Yes   No

7. It's really unfair to my boyfriend to spend time with my friends.

Yes   No

8. I feel hesitant to be as friendly as I used to be with my other guy friends.

Yes   No

9. My boyfriend is easily upset. I need to find just the right way to say what I mean.

Yes   No

10. Our relationship isn't becoming easier, gentler, and kinder.

Yes   No

11. My spiritual life is just not progressing, but it'll get better.

Yes   No

12. He sees his interests as more important than mine.

Yes   No

13. I find myself making excuses for him, for example: "He's just not that kind of guy. He'll get better."

Yes   No

14. My goals and meaning in life seem to be replaced with my desire to keep him happy.

Yes   No

15. I wonder why my parents and friends don't understand what a great guy he really is. They're usually better at judging character.

    Yes   No

9

Is This a Mutual Relationship?

> **To:** Paige@College.com
> **From:** Dad@HarveyHome.com
> **Subject:** Detecting a theme

Dear Paige,

Well, I think I'm starting to hear a theme in the problems you've had with the last two guys you've dated. And I think it explains why you couldn't get to a point of feeling at ease with them. Does the phrase, "You're investing a hundred dollars in a two-dollar relationship," mean anything to you? That's what you were doing, and I think you came to the same conclusion.

First, there was Gary. Now, he was a really nice guy. He treated you about as nice as you could ever hope to be treated. (I like to see that in the guys you date.) He was courteous, respectful, attentive—all the things that make you feel special. But he was also a private person. Did I say private? Gary

To: Paige@College.com
Date: Dad@HarveyHome.com
Subject: Detecting a theme

wouldn't know an emotion if it bit him, much less have the ability to talk about it! You would talk about how you were feeling, and Gary would just go silent on you. He didn't know what to say or do. What was it you said . . . sometimes you'd just "complete his sentences" for him? So you shared and shared—and you expected him to do the same. But you got nothing in return. I know that frustrated you; it probably would frustrate anybody. Gary had his plusses, but he also had his limitations. So what you had together couldn't get past a superficial level. You two weren't "mutual" when it came to sharing.

Then there was Clark—another nice guy. (I've noticed you tend to only date nice guys.) But he didn't want to deal with personal stuff, either. Now, he was a little more direct about it. Gary would just go blank when you started getting into personal stuff. You knew the conversation was over because his lips stopped moving. Clark would at least tell you he wasn't going

To: Paige@College.com
From: Dad@HarveyHome.com
Subject: Detecting a theme

to talk about it. What was his famous line? "That's the kind of stuff you talk about after you're married." This "stuff" was things like your beliefs about God, your experience with God, your dreams and goals about life, the issues that bother you on a day-to-day basis . . . It was OK to talk about sports. But if it had to do with anything personal, it was a premarital taboo. This was another case of nonmutual sharing, and it kept your relationship pretty superficial.

Paige, I think you realized you needed more from a relationship. You're wise enough to know that sharing the things on your heart is something that has to happen if you're going to grow in a relationship. I'm not saying there isn't a place for some privacy. But if sharing isn't taking place, neither is closeness—because they go hand in hand. Healthy relationships are all about growing close. This closeness involves two people who are willing to share—not just one. And you're also smart enough to know that what is will be. If Clark didn't want to get up close

To: Paige@College.com
From: Dad@HarveyHome.com
Subject: Detecting a theme

and personal until after he got married, he probably wasn't going to do it then, either.

What you need is what every relationship needs in order to grow: Not one person but two individuals committed to doing the work. It's got to be mutual. So hold out for that guy who's willing to be mutual with you. That's God's design.

All my love,

Dad

MUTUALITY—IT'S ALL ABOUT EQUAL INVESTMENT

In my e-mail, I told Paige she was investing a hundred dollars in a two-dollar relationship. What I meant by that was she had been doing all the work in the relationship while her two previous boyfriends had done little or nothing. Now, that's not true for every aspect of those relationships; if it were, they wouldn't have lasted as long as they did. At the core, these were two pretty good guys. But in at least one very crucial relational area, Paige's boyfriends weren't investing nearly what they needed to for the relationships to survive.

For a relationship to make it, for it to grow, there has to be some degree of mutuality demonstrated in several key areas. By *mutuality,* I mean that each person must do his or her share of the work and really invest in the relationship. Don't get me wrong. We all have our flaws, and your relationship isn't going to be perfect. So each person's "investment" isn't always going to be exactly equal. But you do need to see that some degree of equality is being shown in a few very crucial areas, or what may start out as love will soon turn into something ugly. One of those crucial areas is *power,* which we just discussed in chapter 8. But there are other areas that are also important. Three of these areas include sharing, give-and-take, and responsibility. Let's see how these areas are being handled in your relationship.

SHARING

At the beginning of a counseling session I like to ask the couple, "So, how have things been?" On this particular evening, the couple was Jason and Trisha. Jason's response was, "Fine." But Trisha's was, "Just OK." They had experienced the same things in their relationship during the past week, yet each had a different slant on what had happened. I asked them to explain the difference.

For Jason, everything depended upon whether or not they argued. So his "Fine" meant there was an absence of conflict, and that's what he wanted most in their relationship. Trisha wanted the calmness too, and she wasn't disagreeing about there not being any arguments during the week. But she wanted more. There hadn't been any arguing, but neither had there been any sharing. So she was feeling disconnected. As she put it, "I feel distant." That's the same feeling Paige experienced (and for the same reason) with the two guys mentioned in my e-mail.

Sharing is all about self-disclosure. It's about looking at what's going on in your heart and soul and then talking about it—sharing what you really think and how you really feel. This needs to be about the important matters in life, matters such as talking about what God is saying to you—or that maybe He's being silent. It's also about sharing your dreams, your fears, your whatever. Sharing your heart enables you to know and to be known. It's what bonds you together. And it's got to happen if you're ever, *ever* going to feel close.

I like to think of "feeling close" as a process. You just don't get it done in one quick and easy step. It takes time. But time alone won't get it done. You have to be doing the right things with your time. People are like onions, not apples. When Paige was young, she liked apples. But she hated the skin, so I would peel an apple before giving it to her. That wasn't a big deal. I mean, hey, it doesn't take much to peel an apple. But try peeling an onion! If you wanted to (and I don't know why you would), you could do it all day. You'd just keep peeling it down, one layer at a time. Well, we're a whole lot more like onions than we are apples. And the process of growing close involves our taking the risk to share how we feel, one layer at a time. Layer by layer, we begin to know, to be known, to trust, to feel closer, and we become even more willing to share again. At least that's what's supposed to happen.

Becoming close is God's great design for marriage. We are created for intimacy and intended to bond. But it takes two people, both taking the risk and doing the work, for it to happen. If you and your boyfriend are both doing your work—if it's mutual—then you know what I'm talking about. But if you're doing all the work by yourself—if he's holding out—you're feeling distant and maybe frustrated.

When sharing isn't mutual, the relationship looks superficial and feels empty. Use the Quick Quiz on Sharing to get a grasp of what's happening in your relationship.

QUICK QUIZ ON SHARING

1. The term that describes how I most often feel in this relationship is
   a. *distant.* We never share, or I'm the one who does all the sharing.
   b. *superficially close.* Physically, we're together a lot, but we don't do a great deal of sharing.
   c. *close.* We both share equally.

2. The term that best describes how often my boyfriend talks with me about personal things is
   a. *never.*
   b. *occasionally* (but not as often as I would like).
   c. *whenever either of us feels the need.*

3. When I try to talk to my boyfriend about emotional things, he
   a. changes the subject.
   b. listens to what I have to say but does not respond.
   c. listens and then responds to what I have to say.

GIVE-AND-TAKE

Do you feel taken advantage of by your boyfriend? If anyone's going to go the extra mile, is it going to have to be you? When it comes to give-and-take, are you all give? Is he all take? Is everything about *him*—is he the center of the universe? If you answered yes to any of these questions, then you're in a nonmutual relationship. You have an imbalance in give-and-take, one of those bedrocks of a relationship. It's got to be there in some form or you're going to crash and burn.

If you're like most people, you want to be a giver, and you enter a relationship willing to do just that. You want to please, to be kind, to show just how much you care. But you give with the anticipation that he is going to do the same right back, that he will sacrifice as much for you as you do for him. It's not really a "bargain," though some people try to portray it that way. It's simply how a relationship is designed to work: two people willingly sacrificing for each other. When your giving is returned, you find yourself continuing to give. *Voilà!* Cooperation and caring break out.

All of that is fine—and as things should be. It's when giving is not returned in an equal measure—when your relationship is nonmutual—that problems begin to pop up. This fact may surprise you: Not every guy is a giver. There are some who don't even start out as givers. But even those who do sometimes just stop putting their best foot forward. They become takers. Then if too many events get scheduled, it will be your activities that get dropped to free up some time, not his. And when you both want to go to different restaurants, you're going to end up going where he wants to go. When he needs your help, you'll be Johnny-on-the-spot to lend a hand. But when you need his help, he'll be too busy with his (more important) life. The balance of the giving and the taking has shifted.

So what happens when giving stops being mutual? Nothing. At least, nothing happens right a way. Remember, you're a giver. You still care about him, and at the core of your very being, you still want to give. Maybe you'll even hold on to the dream that things are going to change, and you'll keep on giving for an even longer time. But eventually you'll tire of the unfairness. That's when you'll really start to get angry, and what was once love will begin to turn to something else.

I'd do anything for Jan—and she knows it. Jan knows that, barring something beyond my control, I'll not only be there for her, I'll show up enthused. You won't see me dragging my feet, complaining, or huffing, groaning, and sighing (making statements without the use of words) about the demands she places on my life. I give joyfully. I want to invest in her life because I love her, and I see marriage as a mutual relationship. The funny thing is, I know she'll be there for me, too. You see, we've both grasped the truth that a good marriage is going to cost each spouse something. And we're both willing to pay the price.

When the give-and-take isn't mutual, the relationship looks selfish and feels frustrating. Use the Quick Quiz on Give-and-Take on page 98 to get a grasp of what's happening in your relationship.

RESPONSIBILITY

I was talking with a tired and frustrated wife recently who began our therapy session with the statement, "I'll raise three kids, but I won't raise four!" She had only three children. The fourth

---

QUICK QUIZ ON GIVE-AND-TAKE

1. The attitude that best describes my boyfriend when I ask him to do something for me is
   a. not interested. If it isn't going to benefit him, he's not going to do it.
   b. a struggle. He'll usually do it, but with lots of sighing.
   c. no problem. He's very willing to go the extra mile for me.

2. When it comes to how my needs count in this relationship, they
   a. don't count at all. (He's going to do what he wants to do, and he gets indignant when I complain.)
   b. count some, but not as much as I would like. (Sometimes he makes adjustments for me, but it's rare.)
   c. count a lot. (My needs are as important to him as his are.)

3. My boyfriend
   a. is pretty self-focused (i.e. expects me to do all the giving).
   b. occasionally sees that the whole world doesn't revolve around him, but that seems to be pretty difficult for him to do. (He prefers that I make all the sacrifices.)
   c. sees us as having a mutual relationship and expects give-and-take on both sides (i.e., he adjusts his schedule for me as much as I do for him).

"child" to whom she was referring was her husband. "I feel more like his mother than I do his wife!" she fumed. By this, she meant she was responsible for too much in his life. She was the primary breadwinner. (He was either unemployed or under-employed.) While running the entire household (he could not be counted on for any help), she somehow managed to also juggle a full-time career and all the childcare. Wow! No wonder she was tired. I got tired just listening to all she had to do. And no wonder she was frustrated. She *was* raising four!

You've read enough in this book to know that problems like this one don't just suddenly emerge in a relationship. There had to have been signs while this couple was dating to indicate his behavior might turn out like this eventually. So I began asking those historical kinds of questions. Sure enough, I wasn't dis-appointed. Even back then, his lack of responsibility had come shining through. Whereas she had completed her degree in four years, he had struggled to cram four years into six. Did I say six? Even then, he did not finish. And with some embarrassment, she admitted that this had happened—or not happened—even with her helping. "I did a lot of his papers. I thought it would help him to get through. But nothing seemed to really work."

I'm not going to go into all the clinical issues that could have been going on here, some of it for a long, long time. I only want to point out that this is a pretty good example of what mutual responsibility is *not*. When you're acting responsibly, you're taking care of yourself, and you're pitching in to pull your share of the load for the relationship as well. In this situation, she's doing all the work: hers, his, and theirs. She's the one who has to step up if things are going to get done—even everyday things. And he just lets her do it. She *is* his mother! And she probably could have seen it coming a mile away—if she'd only thought about it.

What does it look like when you're more of a mother than a girlfriend? Let's see. Are you his memory? Is it your job to remind him of where he's supposed to be, what he's supposed to be doing, when and why? And of course, when he forgets to actually do it, do you do it for him? Are you his accountability partner? Is it your job to keep him straight—to tell him what he can and cannot do? Does he call upon you to make his decisions for him? Are you the worker bee? If it gets done, is it because you see to it? This includes jobs he's supposed to do, like picking up the dry cleaning or running by the store (or writing papers for class).

But it's more than just what you do for him. It also includes things in your relationship. If you're going out to that special restaurant, will it happen if you don't make the reservations? If you stopped "doing" in this relationship, would it even continue? Are you the reason the two of you are still an item? If any of this is true, then you're in a nonmutual relationship, and you're working way too hard!

When responsibility isn't mutual, the relationship looks irresponsible and feels exasperating. Use the Quick Quiz on Responsibility on the facing page to get a grasp of what's happening in your relationship.

QUICK QUIZ ON RESPONSIBILITY

1. If anything gets done in our relationship (like planning for our dates and time together), it's because
   a. I step in and take care of it.
   b. I remind him enough until he finally steps up and does it.
   c. we both share in seeing that things get done.

2. When assessing my role in this relationship, I most often feel like
   a. a mother.
   b. a cheerleader.
   c. a partner.

3. The word that best describes how I feel in this relationship is:
   a. *frustrated* by his irresponsible behavior.
   b. *overwhelmed* from having to pull more than my fair share of the load.
   c. *comfortable* because we both take responsibility in this relationship.

To: Paige@College.com
From: Dad@HarveyHome.com
Subject: Ought to versus have to

Dear Paige,

OK, let me see if I've got this straight. You're mad at John. Not because he's mad at you, but because you can't get him to talk to you about whatever it is that's made him mad. Seems like I've heard this story before with John. Does he still do the wounded-guy routine? You know, the one where he gets silent and pouts and mopes around for a while. That used to make you feel pretty guilty and hooked you into pursuing him— you "tried to get him to open up." Maybe his pulling back doesn't affect you that way anymore. Since you've seen this routine before, you're probably feeling tired and frustrated rather than guilty.

Well, you ought to be getting tired of it. And

To: Paige@College.com
From: Dad@HarveyHome.com
Subject: Ought to versus have to

I agree with what you said: "We should be able to just talk about it when we're mad at each other without him getting his feelings hurt." You ought to. This routine you two are in has concerned me for quite a while. You see, Paige, it's more than an "ought" to—it's a "have" to. You both have to be able to deal with the problems that come up between you—the frustrations, the hurts, the disappointments—and get to some kind of resolution, or there's going to be nothing but hard times in your future.

I know it's not fun to talk about being mad. But let's face it: There are no perfect relationships, and every couple has to talk about their problems. Sooner or later, one of you is going to say something you shouldn't, or not say something you should, or have something that was said innocently be totally misinterpreted. The result? Hurt feelings. Or one of you is going to do something you shouldn't do, or not do something you should do, or have something that you do completely taken the wrong way. Frustration and disappointment are just a matter of time.

To: Paige@College.com
From: Dad@HarveyHome.com
Subject: Ought to versus have to

To top it off, most of this will be unintentional. Still, you'll end up getting mad at the person you care about the most.

There's no easy answer. And I know that when you're angry it seems real appealing to just not deal with it. But if you don't deal with your anger, the problems don't get fixed and the emotions can't go away. Like the proverbial snowball rolling down the hill, your problems will only get bigger and bigger.

You and John have a snowball kind of relationship. The issues between you are getting bigger and bigger. I know that's not the kind of relationship you want with John—even though it's what you seem to have at present. But things can change. Know what you need—a boyfriend who will deal with you when he's angry—and don't settle for anything less. You're right to be frustrated with what's happening, and your problems are too important to simply let go.

You make me proud to be a dad.

Dad

IF YOU WANT TO BE CLOSE . . .

Let me tell you one thing you can count on in your relationship: It will not be frustration-free. I don't care how well matched you are, you're going to say or do something that will hurt your boyfriend's feelings. No matter how perfect he thinks you are, you're going to disappoint him. And I don't care how nice you are, you're going to make him mad. So the big question is not whether this is going to happen but what are you going to do when it does? If you want a growing relationship, you're going to have to live by this relationship golden rule: *If it's significant enough to get upset about (or bothered by), then it's important enough to deal with.*

Why all the fuss? Why is dealing with conflicts such a big deal? Because you don't want to face the consequences if you don't. You're supposed to be growing closer together, and that's not going to happen if you don't deal with conflict. If you don't deal with the things that come up between the two of you, you won't have resolution. If you can't get resolution, walls start getting erected between you and your boyfriend. After the walls are built, you will start feeling resentful and begin to push each other away. It's as simple as that. So if you want to be close, you're going to have to deal with your conflicts.

PRINCIPLES FOR LIVING

The Bible wasn't intended to give you specific advice on every possible situation you might face in life, but it does give you some pretty clear principles for living. And when you look at the way Jesus conducted relationships in His own life, you begin to develop some sound guidelines for your own. Let's look at some of the guidelines that directly deal with conflict.

Be honest and speak the truth

I have found Christians to be some of the most dishonest people I know. Not because they steal things or take advantage of others, but because they lie about their feelings. We might be mad enough to spit nails, but rather than dealing with our anger, we put on that smile and go on as if nothing has happened. Instead of hiding these feelings, Paul tells us to "speak the truth" to each other (Ephesians 4:25).

That should be enough of a directive. But in addition Jesus demonstrated this principle as a lifestyle. He never shied away from sharing what He believed or how He felt, even when He knew that not everyone would appreciate it. Sometimes He infuriated those around Him (see Luke 4:28). Was it His goal to hurt people's feelings? Absolutely not—He was the compassionate Savior. But it was His goal to be honest. It was the best way, so He did it in spite of the consequences.

Realize that anger is not sin

The Bible says it's possible to be angry without sinning. Whew! That's good to know. Paul made this advice clear when he said, "If you are angry, do not let anger lead you into sin" (Ephesians 4:26 NEB). He was telling us we can feel anger (an emotion) and yet not commit sin (what we do with it).

There is nothing wrong with anger. It is a God-given emotion with a purpose. It lets you know when there's something you don't like—and it gives you momentum to deal with it. *Mishandling* anger is what gets you into trouble.

Deal quickly with your anger

Again, it's Paul who gives direction on dealing with anger. He said, "Do not let sunset find you still nursing it [anger]" (Ephesians 4:27 NEB). There are good reasons for dealing quickly with anger. First, let's face it: It's not going to go away on its own. It's just going to stay there and fester until you deal with it. So why waste all that valuable time being mad? Just deal with your anger and move on with your life. But also, if you don't deal with your anger—if you continue to "nurse" it—it can morph into something very different. It turns into resentment. Whereas anger is a healthy God-given emotion, resentment is malignant. It sours our attitudes and warps our vision of each other. (I define resentment as "anger with a history.")

So, what is the godly way of handling anger? Deal with it honestly, appropriately, directly, and quickly. Why? Because it's the best thing you can do for your relationship, and it's one of the ways the two of you can grow closer together.

WHAT DOES AVOIDANCE LOOK LIKE?

Whenever you do something to avoid dealing with how you really feel, you are being emotionally dishonest. Avoidance rarely solves a problem. Sooner or later the unresolved issues will arise again, perhaps with even greater potential to damage your relationship. Avoidance can occur in several different forms. I'll describe some of its more common manifestations to help you identify whether they may be operating in your current relationship.

Stuffing

When you become angry or hurt but you just keep those feelings to yourself, you're stuffing your emotions. For example, let's say you said something that hurt your boyfriend's feelings, and instead of talking to you about it, he avoided the issue by stuffing his feelings and acting as though nothing had happened. Now, he might tell himself something like, *What she said doesn't really matter; I'll get over it.* But it *does* matter.

Stuffing may *seem* better than dealing directly with an emotional issue, but it isn't. In this illustration, your boyfriend can only stuff his feelings for so long before his emotions just have to come out. And when they do, *wow!* It's an explosion. There's nothing pretty—or redeeming—about such a scene. Deal with your feelings before they get volatile. Don't stuff them away.

Denial

"Me, mad? No, I'm not mad. What makes you think I'm mad?" Well, maybe because of your red face or your clenched fists or the way you're gritting your teeth, and oh yeah, your jaw is clamped shut. Your lips may be saying one thing, but your body is telling an entirely different story. Sometimes denial means you're *lying to yourself,* maybe trying to convince yourself that you're not angry. At other times, denial means you're *lying to others.* You know you're mad, but you think you can hide your anger from everyone else. The predictable thing about anger is, it won't stay bottled up. It always finds a way to get out.

Changing the subject

Let's say you're out on a date and your boyfriend does something that really hurts you. Being a fairly intelligent guy, he figures out what's going on. He knows you want to talk to him about your hurt feelings, but he becomes real uncomfortable with where your conversation is going. So he does the ol' change-up on you and asks, "So, um, what did you think of that movie?" If he's really good at this technique, he'll allow a little strategic pause between your statement and his (worth nine out of ten possible skill points). But you're probably getting my point. If you allow him to change the subject, the issue is successfully avoided—but it remains unresolved and will continue to be a barrier between the two of you.

Withdrawal

There are several different ways to avoid emotional situations through withdrawal. For example, your boyfriend might withdraw from you by simply being *silent*. He doesn't have to go anywhere; he's still right there beside you. But emotionally he has stepped behind an invisible wall. Add a little drama to the silence, and you'll get a *pout*. Your boyfriend may do this to let you know he's not happy but still does not want to talk about it. He may even suck you in a little closer with a strategy that causes you to try to "get him" to talk about it. Smooth, huh?

Then there's the more classic form of withdrawal where he

does leave. He might simply move to another room, or he could walk out. In a more dramatic technique, he slams the door of his truck and then peels out, throwing gravel for half a mile. If you've dated a guy for any length of time, you're probably seen withdrawal in one form or another.

Passive–aggressive withdrawal

When your boyfriend is avoiding an issue through passive-aggressive withdrawal, he's mad and he's going to get at you, but he's not going to do it directly. So instead of talking to you about how his feelings are hurt, he starts complaining about your cat or about how something you did was really stupid or . . . Now, there's nothing wrong with your cat, and what you did wasn't really all that stupid. He's just mad. He may not even know why he's mad. But one thing he does know: He's not going to talk to you directly about the issue that has caused the problem.

Getting really upset

"Now you've done it! Now I'm really ticked!" To effectively shut down a conversation and avoid the elephant hiding under the carpet, this statement has to be made in a loud voice with all the appropriate nonverbal indicators (facial grimaces, hand gestures, body stiffness, skin flushing) that are supposed to accompany a statement of this magnitude. The goal is to strike fear and trembling in your very soul so you will not dare venture into whatever the subject is that's being avoided.

There are times when emotions run so high that a time-out is exactly what's needed. But is this a pattern? When your boyfriend repeatedly gets upset because there's no other way to avoid talking about a troubling issue, that pattern of behavior becomes a problem for your relationship.

So let's review what needs to be happening in your relationship to bring you and your boyfriend closer:

- You need to be able to deal with your disappointments.

- You need to be able to discuss your disagreements.

- You need to be able to share your hurts.

And you need to do all this dealing and discussing and sharing even though it's not always easy to do.

Let me be the first to admit that dealing with anger isn't easy. And as I've talked to guys (and girls) who have struggled with this dealing, I've found that there isn't one reason for the difficulty. Sometimes a guy avoids dealing with his feelings for *self-protective* reasons. He fears disappointing you and worries what you might think of him if he really says what he thinks. The last thing any guy wants is rejection.

Sometimes he's motivated by his attempt at being *overprotective*. Instead of fearing what *you* might say to *him*, he simply wants to avoid situations when he might say anything that could hurt your feelings. I call this *over*protective because healthy people not only take responsibility for how they feel, but they allow others to do the same.

Sometimes the problem is some form of *misbelief* about what he's supposed to do in a relationship. Maybe he thinks he's doing the "Christian" thing by not talking about his anger. And maybe he just never learned how to do it right—to express anger or share hurt feelings in nondestructive ways. Remember, we learn a lot from our home life, and not all of it's helpful.

The bottom line is this: Dealing with your feelings can be difficult (for a variety of reasons), but that doesn't change the *need* for you to deal with your conflicts. You have to get it done despite the difficulties. If you can't deal with the normal things in life that come up between the two of you, you'll erect walls in your relationship and become resentful. After a while, you won't really like each other very much. And that's not how healthy relationships are designed.

11

Is He Mr. Right, or Am I Settling for Less Than I Deserve?

To: Paige@College.com
From: Dad@HarveyHome.com
Subject: Passion

Dear Paige,

Well, I must say that your comment last night is one of the more interesting things I've heard in a while. Let me see. I think it went something like this: "Over the last six months, there's been more passion in your and Mom's relationship than in John's and mine."

First of all, you don't know the level of passion in our relationship! I know what you *think* you know—and I find that a little insulting! But I was able to get past the insult to realize that your statement wasn't really about us, but about you and John. And the more I thought about what you were really saying, the more I didn't like what I was hearing.

Another statement you made has reinforced

To: Paige@College.com
From: Dad@HarveyHome.com
Subject: Passion

my concern. You told me, "He's a great guy—but I want to feel 'giddy' about him. Is that too much to ask for?" To answer your question, no, I don't think wanting to feel giddy is too much to ask. Now understand, a relationship has to have a whole lot more going for it than just emotion. Sometimes we put too much weight in just how we "feel" about someone. That's especially true when feelings are the *only* things that seem to count. But a relationship that's leaning toward permanence ought to have at least a strong emotional base.

I'm not exactly sure what *giddy* means to you. But I think you ought to be at least *enthused* about each other. Seeing him ought to do something to you. Talking to him ought to do something to you. Having to be apart from each other ought to do something to you. And if these things aren't doing much to you—if either of you feels less than enthused about the other—then there really *is* something wrong.

Paige, I'm not talking "against" John. I like him and think he's a great guy. I could get

To: Paige@College.com
From: Dad@HarveyHome.com
Subject: Passion

used to having him around at Thanksgiving every year. For that matter, I'm not talking against anyone else either (though there are some guys you've dated that I probably could talk against). But that's not the point here. What I am doing now is talking "for" something. And that something is this: *You ought to feel passionate about the one you love.* If you don't feel this passion, then maybe he's not the one for you. He could be a lot of things to you. He could be a close friend or a confidant. But he's not going to be your soul mate.

God only has the best in mind for you! That's true for every aspect of your life—including marriage. He never asks you to "settle" on anything. So you can be certain that He's not leading you to settle on something as important as a life partner. You're right to have some concerns. So trust your instinct, take your time, and don't rush into any major decision. There's too much at stake.

Seeing you grow in wisdom,

Dad

IN SEARCH OF MR. RIGHT

A colleague recently wrote that if you're having a difficult time finding "Mr. Right," you might want to consider looking for "Mr. OK" or "Mr. Pretty Good." I chuckled the first time I read that statement. But the more I thought about it, the more I didn't like it. I don't want *my* daughter marrying Mr. OK or Mr. Pretty Good. I don't even want her dating those guys! I don't want her marrying Mr. Pretty Darn Close. I only want Paige marrying Mr. Right—*her* Mr. Right. And I believe there's someone out there who meets that description.

Now, it may be that my colleague was trying to say there are some women who do place their expectations pretty high— maybe too high. They are picky, picky, picky! No man could ever meet the expectations these ladies have set for Mr. Right. Sometimes when people are *afraid* of relationships—or better yet, afraid of getting hurt in relationships—having extremely high standards keeps them safe. There isn't anyone good enough for them to date! Other times, excessive pickiness results from being extremely self-centered. When you're selfish, it's not easy to find someone who can meet all your needs all the time.

So I guess there is such a thing as looking for Mr. Too Right. But when you compare the problem of either being too picky or not being picky enough, it has been my experience that people are much likelier to "get into the boat" far too soon by settling than they are to miss the boat altogether by wanting too much. *Settling* is a bigger problem.

SETTLING

When I use the interesting term *settling* in regard to a relationship, it always involves a choice that *you* make about *him*—and it's always a choice that has you giving up something important, something you really want (and deserve), in order to keep the relationship—even an otherwise "pretty good" relationship.

Don't get me wrong. Not everyone settles. Some girls get what they want. They have *arrived* at their destination—they've waited on Mr. Right. Not willing to sacrifice what's important (the big-ticket items) by settling for another person, they have processed, evaluated, let some relationships go, moved on to others. They have waited until things were right for them. Others are doing what I call the "good work"—they are on the *journey* to their destination. Still in the process of making a good lovedecision, they may not have found what they want, but neither have they settled for what they *don't* want.

In all these cases, whether settling, finding, or still searching, each stage boils down to a choice you're making about your relationship. If your boyfriend's not measuring up in the important things in your life—the things you really need from your Mr. Right—you have to ask yourself a serious question: *Is he really worth what I'm choosing to give up?*

COMMON CONFUSION ABOUT MR. RIGHT

There is a common confusion about Mr. Right. I know this because I've heard the same questions from women over and over again. You're probably asking them, too.

Is there one and only one Mr. Right?

I know it sounds romantic to think there is one perfect person out there who is just waiting to discover you. When I think of my own marriage, I like to think that Jan is the only one who could possibly have been my perfect match. But my more rational self knows that this probably isn't a realistic thought.

Though there are lots and lots of guys who are Mr. Wrong, there's also more than one—though obviously a much smaller number—who could be Mr. Right. These are guys with whom you would have a mutual attraction, a mutual willingness to commit and invest, a mutual level of emotional well-being, a mutual fit on the important issues in life. I'm using a lot of qualifiers here—and putting a heavy emphasis on *mutual*—but you get the point. There aren't going to be a lot of guys who measure up to your standards, but there'll be more than one.

Is anyone truly perfect?

When you start off with an image of what your Mr. Right will be like—your ideal image—several things go into that descriptive buildup. To name just a few, you may have an ideal physical image in mind—height, weight, build, hair color. You probably have given some thought to his personality—outgoing, humorous, easygoing. Your Mr. Right will also have a certain set of values and beliefs—typically exactly like yours. Your ideal image of Mr. Right will encompass many different things. Can anybody ever truly and perfectly match such an ideal?

Probably not. But what often happens is this: After meeting someone you really begin to care for, you find that either your image of what is ideal changes, or you find that some of those things just don't seem to matter anymore. Maybe you wanted someone tall, dark, and handsome, and though Mr. Potentially Right is still good-looking to you, he may not make it as a model for one of those clothing magazines. But that's OK.

The important thing to realize is that although there will not be a perfect fit with your ideal image of Mr. Right, there are big-ticket items and little-ticket items that present choices for you. You have to decide what's truly important to you and what is not. Hair color may not be that big a deal, but what about his religious preference? Be sure to hold on to the big-ticket qualities. When your ideal image of Mr. Right begins to change through the elimination of the really important stuff, you've begun to settle.

Does this make him a bad person?

Deciding your boyfriend is not Mr. Right isn't necessarily about deciding he should be labeled as good or bad. As we've already discussed, there are some guys who aren't right for anybody—who simply aren't marriageable. And there are some men out there who might be thought of as bad people. But determining that your boyfriend isn't Mr. Right isn't saying either of these things about him. He may be a great guy. He's just not Mr. Right *for you.*

Settling is usually an issue of "fit." Paige has dated several guys who were nice enough, but I've questioned whether they were a good fit. With many of these guys, I may have liked *him*—but I didn't like *them*. I didn't like the way he and Paige related to each other. The same may be true with you. You have probably dated guys who were marriageable—who definitely could be Mr. Right for somebody—just not you. What's important is that *he is Mr. Right for you.*

A MARRYING KIND OF LOVE

So, let's get back to wanting to feel "giddy." Is there anything wrong with wanting to feel passionate toward your boyfriend—or being concerned when you're not feeling much at all? First of all, let me offer a disclaimer: You're not going to feel anything—no matter what the emotion—all the time. Human beings are too complex, and so is life, for that to happen. There are too many factors influencing us on a moment-to-moment basis. So the real issue is not necessarily how do you feel about your boyfriend every moment you're together but what is the pervasive theme of your feelings? Generally, do you feel passionate or passionless? That's the real question.

According to Dr. Robert Sternberg of Yale University, that pervasive theme of your feelings—how you feel toward your boyfriend overall—is extremely important. In fact, without passion, Sternberg would say you don't really have a *marrying* kind of love. You might have some other kind of love—like *friendship* love, or *liking* love—but you don't have a marrying kind of love.

Now, that's not exactly the terminology that Sternberg uses, but it's close. Sternberg studied relationships and found that there are three elements in true love. (Sternberg's term for true love is *consummate* love.) He suggests that true love has a balance between *passion* (physical attraction), *intimacy* (affection, mutual disclosure, closeness), and *commitment* (a conscious decision to love, share, and be together). The kind of love your relationship has is then determined by what combination of these three elements you possess. If your relationship has two of the three, let's say, intimacy and commitment, but it lacks passion, then Sternberg says you have a *companionate* (friendship) love. Your boyfriend may be a great guy, but he will feel more like your brother than your lover.

Sternberg's model is an interesting way to assess your relationship. He describes eight different kinds of love that are derived from putting these three elements together in all their possible combinations. Our focus here is not about all the different possible kinds of love. Instead we're identifying what qualifies as "settling" in your relationship. One extremely important aspect of determining whether you're settling comes from looking at passion and trying to determine whether it's legitimate for you to want to feel passionate toward your boyfriend. Does giving up passion mean you're settling? Sternberg seems to be answering that for a healthy relationship, you and your boyfriend ought to have at least three things going for you—and one of them has to be passion. If not, he's not your Mr. Right, and you are settling for a lesser kind of love.

IS HE MR. RIGHT?

So how do you know if he's Mr. Right? I guess it gets down to your asking a few questions about yourself and your relationship: First, *Do you know what qualities are really important to you?* These are the big-ticket items for your life (the legitimate things that you just have to have in a relationship). Next, *Are you getting these things from your boyfriend?* For example, do you feel passionately toward him? Last, *Have you spent enough time together to know these things for sure?*

When he's *your* Mr. Right, you'll be comfortable with his behavior instead of worrying about what he might say or do. You'll feel confident about your shared values instead of worrying about them being compromised. You'll be comfortable with your beliefs instead of constantly waiting for them to be called into question. There'll be no question about how you feel toward him: You will be passionate. And you won't have to give up anything that you really need because you'll be getting everything you deserve.

12

Am I Number One?

To: Paige@College.com
From: Dad@HarveyHome.com
Subject: Don and Jamie

Dear Paige,

I saw your friends Don and Jamie last night. It's been a year since I last saw them, and it surprised me to find out just how much has changed in their lives. You remember how Don was the youth pastor at a large church when he and Jamie married a few years ago? Well, last year he became the senior (and only) pastor of a small church in a rural town about an hour away. Talk about culture shock! The move meant Jamie had to change jobs. She went from being a computer analyst with a large corporation to working in a rural school system. To top it all off, Jamie is pregnant, and the two of them will soon become the *three* of them. Wow! That's a lot of changes.

lovedecisions

To: Paige@College.com
From: Dad@HarveyHome.com
Subject: Don and Jamie

The one thing that hasn't changed though is just how much they still care for each other. I could tell this in just a few minutes by watching the way they treated each other. You know—the little things. There's a kindness to their touch and a close attentiveness when the other person speaks. Don kinda summed up what I was sensing in a comment he made to Jamie: "You know, out of all the people in this town, I like you the best." Then he smiled. He wasn't really limiting his comparison to just the people in that little rural town. And Jamie knew it. He wasn't comparing her to anyone at all. It was just his humorous way of saying that, to him, Jamie is the number one person is his life, regardless of the context.

I don't want to make too much out of one comment. But I don't want to make too little of it, either. Don truly loves Jamie. He knows she is the best thing that ever happened to him, and he wants *her* to know she's the best thing that ever happened to him. So he intentionally communicates this in both the

126

To: Paige@College.com
From: Dad@HarveyHome.com
Subject: Don and Jamie

little things and the big things that he does. I think Jamie is getting the message. And knowing that she's Don's number one really affects how she feels and relates to him.

Paige, you deserve to be somebody's number one. I don't think that's happened yet. But I know it can. You deserve the best. So don't ever settle for less. You won't start off as number one in a relationship. That's OK. Real love takes time. But as things move along, if feeling like you're number one isn't a part of the equation, then that relationship isn't for you. Your mother's my number one—and I'm hers. You won't be happy unless someone feels the same way about you.

You'll always be number one to me.

Dad

"I DON'T FEEL CHERISHED"

Jason and Kathy had been in a relationship for several years. They had talked about marriage a couple of times, but it just seemed to be too big a step for them to take. Finally sensing the need to either move in one direction or the other (either get married or move on with their lives separately), they came for some help in making "the big decision."

Both agreed they did not "feel close" in the relationship and that this feeling of distance played a big part in their hesitancy to marry. It made them wonder if they were really right for each other. Several things struck me about them. They had very different personalities as well as different values and beliefs. These differences alone would make the ease of connecting more difficult. Much of what seemed to have kept them together for this long was just the comfort of being a couple. But relationships are complex, and I didn't want to oversimplify their situation by jumping to any premature conclusions. So we continued to talk about what concerned them. Eventually Kathy identified what was, for her, the real heart of the matter when she said, "I don't feel cherished by Jason."

In the last chapter when I asked you to question whether you were settling for less than you deserved, the focus was on how *you* feel about *him*. In this chapter, the focus shifts to something equally important. Now I want to know your perception of how *he* feels about *you*.

That was Kathy's concern. She cared for Jason but had found that her willingness to make *him* number one had not resulted in his making *her* number one. Fluctuating between feeling hurt, confused, and frustrated, she began to protect herself by pulling back emotionally. However, distance was not what she wanted in a relationship, and the more time that passed, the more anxious and unsettled she became. Jason was content for things to rock along in noncommittal mode. But, ready for relief, it was Kathy who finally forced the issue.

EVERYBODY DESERVES TO BE SOMEBODY'S NUMBER ONE

If you don't get anything else from this chapter, at least get this: *You deserve to be his number one priority.* That's the way we're wired. Some colleagues of mine, Leslie Greenberg and Susan Johnson, said it this way in their book, *Emotionally Focused Therapy for Couples:* "The marital relationship provides the opportunity for interdependence, the chance to have one's feelings and needs respected, and the opportunity to be the most important person to a significant other."

I know that sounds a little clinical, but they're echoing the scriptural model. Remember the Genesis 2:24 passage? "Therefore a man *leaves* his father and his mother and *cleaves* to his wife" (italics mine). I stressed the *leaving* portion earlier because that has to happen before you can even think about bonding with someone else. But God's grand design for marriage is that you do bond to that "significant other." That can only happen when you feel cherished, special, and prioritized. The apostle Paul knew this. That's why he said men are to love their wives as Christ loved the church. And how did Christ love the church? He gave His life for it (see Ephesians 5:25). If you don't feel like you're number one in his life, you will not trust that he will watch out for your best interests. And without that kind of trust, there will be no closeness.

AM I NUMBER ONE?

So, how can you tell if you're number one? (As a disclaimer, you have to realize you can't be the "only" thing in your boyfriend's life. There has to be a balance.) There are many ways. Here are a few of them:

Are you competing for his time?

Time is a commodity that we seem to have less and less of. We're working longer and harder than ever before, and we have more distractions, from our hobbies to our social lives. There are a million ways to keep busy. But we prioritize what we do and spend our time either *with someone* or *doing something* that is important to us. If you're not getting enough of your boyfriend's time, *who* or *what* is getting more? That's how you determine whether you are a priority.

Comments from girls who are competing for their boyfriend's time sound like this: "He's always busy doing something else, and I only get the leftovers." "If we spend time together it's because I tag along with him and his friends." These girls don't want all their boyfriend's time. They just want what's theirs. They want to count more than his hobbies and his friends. They want to be number one.

Are you competing for his heart?

Here's a typical situation for one couple I meet with, Mary and Jake. Mary wants to spend time with Jake, so she suggests they go to a movie together. Jake responds, "All right, all right. If that's what you want, we'll go to a movie. Just get off my back about it, OK?" So they go to a movie. But for some reason, Mary isn't very satisfied. Jake figures this out, and now Mary has to listen to Jake's complaints about his never being able to satisfy her. "I just can't do enough to please you," he says.

So what happened between Mary and Jake? Mary got Jake's time—but she did not get his heart. The way she expressed it to me was this: "He *appeases* me—but he does not *value* me."

Not having your boyfriend's heart isn't always as obvious as it was with Mary and Jake. One girl unhappily defined her situation this way: "I may get his body, but his mind is somewhere else." Though he spent time with her, his mind always seemed to be preoccupied with other things. His behavior was subtler than Jake's, but his emotional absence was just as noticeable. "He's here—but not really," she said. The funny thing is that we usually know the difference. And *the* difference makes *a* difference.

Are the things that are important to you also important to him?

OK, now I'm not suggesting that your boyfriend take up gardening, or hang gliding, or mountain climbing just because these are things that you are into. It's not a bad idea that you have some interests in common. But that's not what I'm emphasizing here. This is about acknowledgment, support, and valuing. Though he may not have a personal interest in any of these things, because they are important to you and you are important to him, the things you value will also become important to him.

This feeling of acceptance and support is in sharp contrast to having the things you value discounted or put down as being unimportant. Being supported in the things you deem important is part of what makes you feel number one.

Are your concerns being heard?

"When I talk to Jimmy about how I'm really feeling, he just blows me off!" Judy was pretty angry when she told me this. In counselor talk, I'd say Jimmy wasn't "hearing" what Judy had to say. Sure, he was hearing her words. But he wasn't hearing Judy's heart. He was denying the importance of her concerns or discounting them altogether. Sometimes this discounting is obvious; that's when you hear a statement like, "You shouldn't feel like that." At other times, your concerns are discounted more subtly, perhaps with a rolling of the eyes or that little grin that says, *right—ha, ha, ha.* Either way, you don't feel heard.

When you're number one, your concerns matter. Your boyfriend hears more than your words. You are treated with respect. He listens for understanding and hears your heart, validating what you think, feel, and say. You feel heard.

Is he interested in you?

What makes you feel cherished in your relationship? That's a question I asked a group of young women. Though there were several things that told them they were number one in their relationships, there was one thing that was on all their lists: *Their boyfriends demonstrated a genuine interest in them as individuals.* "Brian really likes me, and he intentionally works hard at us being friends," one young woman said. "There is no question in my mind that Tim is really committed to my emotional well-being. He supports me in the things I want to do and my growth as a person," said another. "Chuck slows down from his hectic world to really listen to what I have to say," said a third.

Taking time to listen even when his time is tight says, *You are important to me.* His really wanting to know what's going on in your life says, *You are important to me.* Wanting the best for you even when it may inconvenience him says, *You are important to me.* Liking who you are and wanting to be your friend says, *You are important to me.* All these actions communicate that he's interested in you—and that you're number one to him.

ARE YOU *SPECIAL?*

If I put a fill-in-the-blank statement in front of you and asked you to tell me what your boyfriend does that makes you feel special (I know I'm special because _____), what would you say? There's not just one answer to this question. If you're number one, being special is conveyed in a lot of things he says and does. But what makes these things distinctive is that *they are reserved for just you.* As one girl put it, "I know I'm special because there are some things that he *does* with only me." She was referring to his being attentive and affectionate. There are boundaries when it comes to showing affection, and there's a familiarity of touch that's reserved for only "the intimate one" in your life—and no one else.

Another way you know you're special is by the personal things he *shares* only with you. As a relationship develops, you move from the superficial to the more personal. So part of defining this relationship (and you) as special is hearing things that are meant for your ears only—personal and private things that are "just between us."

Changing the focus a bit, you also know you're special because of the things he *says about you* to others. Does he say good things to his friends? Are you presented to others as being special to him—and unique in your ways? Does he share why he likes you so much? Or does he complain about your shortcomings and joke with his friends about silly things you do? Are you the brunt of his comments? Once again, *the* difference makes *a* difference.

YOU DESERVE TO BE SOMEBODY'S NUMBER ONE

I remember something Paige said after she got off the phone with one of her good friends. Her comment was, "I want someone like Matt. I always feel so good after talking to him." I knew what she meant. Sure, Matt was a good listener. But he did more than listen. Paige knew that what she said counted with Matt. She was validated in every way. That's what she wants from the number one person in her life. That's what she deserves. And it's what you deserve . . . nothing less than being his number one.

TAKE THE RELATIONSHIP QUIZ

Now that you're familiar with what healthy relationships are supposed to look like, you can take the Relationship Quiz to find out if there's trouble in your "paradise." The questions will seem familiar to you. That's because they touch on the important aspects of relationships you've read about in the previous chapters. Taking the Relationship Quiz is a tangible way to take a closer look at your own relationship.

RELATIONSHIP QUIZ

In each of the following statements and questions, select the response that best describes how you feel about your boyfriend and/or your relationship.

1. Being in this relationship has
    a. not been good for me. (Why does loving him make me feel so bad?)

---

b. confused me. (Sometimes I feel good about us—and other times I don't.)

c. helped me. (Being with my boyfriend has helped me to be a better person.)

2. When it comes to how we relate in this relationship,
   a. everything's a struggle.
   b. we still have the same old arguments and issues.
   c. we have less to argue about, and we're feeling really comfortable together.

3. When it comes to the issue of control and making decisions,
   a. I have little or no say in what happens.
   b. my boyfriend listens to me but believes it's he who makes the final decision.
   c. we make decisions jointly. I have just as much say as he does.

4. When it comes to working on our relationship, such as planning dates and other times together, the role I usually take on is
   a. mother. If I left it up to him, nothing would ever get accomplished.
   b. cheerleader. If I remind him enough, he'll finally take some responsibility.
   c. partner. We both take responsibility and see to it that we spend time together.

5. When I try to talk with my boyfriend about emotional things, he
   a. changes the subject or avoids me in some other way.
   b. listens to what I have to say but does not respond.
   c. listens and then responds by sharing his own thoughts and feelings.

6. If I had to identify how much my needs count in this relationship, I'd say
   a. he's going to do what he wants to do, no matter what I think or feel.
   b. sometimes he makes adjustments for me, but it seems to sort of put him out.
   c. we have a mutual relationship, and my needs are as important to him as his are.

7. When my boyfriend gets angry (frustrated, hurt, or disappointed),
   a. he stuffs, gets quiet, pulls away, or snaps at me.
   b. he tries to get me to draw it out of him.
   c. we resolve the issues that are bothering him by communicating honestly.

8. When I get honest and assess whether my boyfriend is really what I want and deserve, I believe
   a. there are some things I really need that he can't give me.
   b. he's got a lot of what I want, but there's just something lacking.

    c. when I look at the things that matter to me, what I want, I realize he's "the real deal."

9. Am I growing spiritually?
   a. No. Since becoming involved in this relationship, I've lost my spiritual edge.
   b. I don't know. I'm confused. I don't know if he's helped or hurt.
   c. Yes. My boyfriend has not hampered my growth; if anything, he has helped me.

10. When it comes to how I fit in his list of priorities,
    a. it seems everything's more important to him than I am.
    b. I'm probably up there near the top, just not the most important priority.
    c. I know I'm special, and I'm his number one priority.

Interpreting your responses

You probably don't need much help to determine how well you did in this quiz. But just so there's no confusion, I'll give you a little guidance. To make the scoring easier, I used the same order in all the questions and statements. Of the three choices, *a* is always the least desirable, *b* is a little better, and *c* is always the most desirable.

So, how did you do? Did you have all *c*'s? Were there any *a*'s or *b*'s? Obviously, the more *a*'s and *b*'s you had, the greater concern I would have for your relationship. But even one *a* or *b* is reason enough to take a deeper look at what's happening between you and your boyfriend.

Taking a deeper look can sound a little scary. You may be wondering just where this searching might lead. I'm certainly not suggesting that you have to break up with your boyfriend based solely on your responses to this quiz. It may be too early to make that kind of decision. And who knows what kind of changes might occur between now and the next step? But if you had even one *a* or *b*, you need to ask some pretty serious questions about the area in which you're lacking a "best" response. But don't stop with that deeper query into the dark caverns of your relationship. When you find your answers, take action.

What would "action" look like? Well, it could involve clarifying to yourself and your boyfriend what your true needs are and how you feel. That way your boyfriend will know what's expected of him in this relationship. Or it could involve change—altering behaviors you're both used to. It could involve seeing a professional (by yourself or together) so you can sort through some of the tougher issues in your relationship. Or it could mean calling a time-out and spending some time apart—cooling your jets and thinking about what you really want and need. Finally, unfortunately, it could involve ending the relationship—something that tends to strike fear in most people's hearts.

Taking action after that deeper look could involve any of these steps and probably some I haven't listed. The important thing is that you *look* and *act*—don't *deny* and *avoid*. Your lovedecision is just about the most important decision you'll ever make. Make it a good one.

PART 3

WHEN THINGS AREN'T
GOING WELL

13

When Should a Relationship End?

To: Paige@AlmostGraduated.com
From: Dad@HarveyHome.com
Subject: Letting go

Dear Paige,

I know these are difficult times for you. And because I'm your dad, I also know you're probably doing a lot of second-guessing about now, wondering, *Was deciding to place a hold on my relationship with Clark the right thing to do? Should I have waited? Am I being too picky?* These are haunting thoughts.

Talking about you and Clark as a "relationship" has a real sterile sound to it. I know Clark—he's a good person. And what you had together had some very good qualities. That's because you both invested a lot of yourselves into each other's lives. That's also what makes this such a difficult decision. Maybe you're thinking, *After investing all*

To: Paige@AlmostGraduated.com
From: Dad@HarveyHome.com
Subject: Letting go

this time and energy, am I going to lose it all? And what does it mean to take a break? My guess is that's another question you're both asking about now. Whatever it means, I know it sounds risky. Where will it lead? Will it move you to a better place? Or is it just fore-stalling the inevitable—the first step toward ending the relationship? I guess this is one of those situations when only time will tell.

I know you haven't stopped caring for Clark. I can tell this by your tears. My guess is that Clark still cares for you, too. But it wasn't a lack of caring that brought you to this decision in the first place. No. Your decision was in spite of the caring. You finally faced reality and recognized that there were other issues in your relationship—things that didn't need to be there. Amid the myriad of emotions that bathe any intimate relationship, these "other things"—things that you were willing to over-look earlier on—just got too big to ignore. (Incidentally, keeping some rationality in the middle of strong emotional pulls is an indica-tion of maturity. That's a good thing.) Beginning to talk about a permanent

To: Paige@AlmostGraduated.com
From: Dad@HarveyHome.com
Subject: Letting go

commitment probably prompted you both to take a little deeper look at what you really had together.

There are times when some relationships need a reassessment. And there are other times when they simply should be ended. These are never easy decisions to make. Sometimes these decisions are simpler when the love you once had has faded. That's what's known as "falling out of love." It's when you still care—as you and Clark continue to do—that things are the most difficult.

I have confidence in your judgment, Paige. More and more you are doing the right things for the right reasons. You'll work through this situation as well. It wasn't impulse that prompted your decision to take a break, and there's no place for impulse now. Allow yourself the time you need in order to feel at peace with whatever decision you end up making.

Increasingly trusting your judgment,

Dad

NOT AN EASY QUESTION—OR AN EASY ANSWER

When should a relationship end? That's a hard question—so hard that I sought help from some real "relationship experts." And who are more expert than those people who are currently in the lovedecisions phase of life? I turned to a group of college students for advice. I asked my students, "When should a relationship end?" Keep in mind that each was currently in a significant relationship. But more importantly, each had also been in a relationship that had not gone the distance.

I was a little hesitant because I had no clue how they would respond. Would the question seem too personal? Would I get only superficial responses? What happened totally amazed me. One by one, these students shared very personal (and complicated) experiences—and then followed them with incredible insights.

Shelly began the discussion with an experience she had with her now–ex-fiancé. She explained to us that after a while it had just become clear that they simply did not share enough in common—at least, enough of the important things. "There are some core things that just have to be there," she told us.

Hearing this, another student, Megan, quickly jumped in and described a past relationship where she could never quite "measure up." Her boyfriend had even told her she was a "nonvirtuous woman" (a nickname we affectionately gave her from that time on). "At that point I realized the problem had more to do with him than with me or even with us—so I broke it off. I just got tired of being controlled."

Wow! That was the response I had been looking for—an intelligent, healthy, young adult perspective on what can typically be a tricky issue to address.

We continued in this vein—one personal experience followed by another—until Brad interrupted the flow of things with one of those questions that was really meant to be more of a statement than a question: "Where does love come in? Doesn't it conquer all?"

Brad's question changed the tone of the conversation. The room grew silent as the students took some time to think through his question from the perspective of their own experience: *Did I really love him? Did I bail out too soon? Should I have stuck it out?* Brad's question was a good one because it led everyone to a very important truth about relationships: Though love is an essential part of any lovedecision, it's not the only part.

IT'S *NOT* ALL ABOUT LOVE

"I really cared for him, but I just came to realize there were some really significant things that were wrong in our relationship." Megan was talking about a specific person, a specific relationship, and very specific "things that were wrong" when she offered her comment. But in a sense she was speaking for everyone else in the room. The theme was the same: "I came to realize . . ."

Choosing to end a relationship is seldom just about love. Of course, there are the exceptions—those times when "you've lost that loving feeling" (to borrow the title of a song first made popular when I was your age). Losing that "loving feeling" makes any decision to break up a little easier. But that's not always the way a relationship ends. Sometimes it happens in spite of just how much you still care about your boyfriend. It's at these times, when you still care, that the decision gets toughest.

INDICATIONS THAT A RELATIONSHIP SHOULD END

When, in spite of love, should a relationship end? There's no easy answer to this question because every relationship is different. But I do have some suggestions that can act as baseline indicators. See how they line up with your past experiences. Better yet, ask yourself if any of these situations describe what's happening in your relationship right now.

You should break off your relationship . . .

1. When you have very different dreams (and goals) for life and marriage

No two people will share exactly the same set of dreams and goals. This is especially true when you recognize that we have both individual dreams (dreams you have for yourself individually) and couple dreams (dreams you have for you both as a couple). Even though relationships can exist with some differences, dreams *have* to have at least some degree of compatibility.

I remember one guy Paige dated, a fella who had a lot going for him—and for them as a couple. But with all they had in common, they also had very different dreams. He dreamed of going home after college—of living in rural America, of having Sunday dinner at his parents' home, of his kids growing up around and playing with their cousins, nieces, and nephews. Paige dreamed of graduate school, metropolitan living, and an opportunity to influence a much larger world. They had very different dreams—and there wasn't much room for compromise. For them to have made it as a couple, someone would have to have given up a dream.

The funny thing about having different dreams is that the problems they create seldom have anything to do with right and wrong. There was nothing wrong with Paige's dream, or for that matter, her boyfriend's dream. The operative word is *difference*. The greater the difference, the harder it is on the relationship.

2. *When you have significant incompatibilities regarding real issues*

There are some things in life that simply don't matter much. The fact that Jan really likes flowers and I don't isn't a big issue in our marriage. But there are other things—like basic values—that are very important. For Christians, something like church affiliation can become a real issue. That's the example Sherry gave.

Sherry's boyfriend, as she shared with our class, was a Christian who had very different beliefs from her own. She thought they could solve their problem by each attending a different church. She even imagined that he might eventually change his beliefs. But he didn't change. And what seemed to be a minor issue at the start of their relationship became increasingly more difficult. "When I finally realized how important it was for us to be able to go to church together, much less to even be able to talk about God, I knew we couldn't make it."

You must have a common ground on the real issues of life. Some things are just too important to give up—even for a relationship—especially when it's yours.

3. *When it seems impossible for your wounds to heal*

Healing is a natural process, and I guess it's true that we can heal from just about any hurt. But there are times in some relationships when it seems that "getting over it" is nearly an impossibility. Often, not being able to heal involves repetitive hurts—and not just one incident. In the case of repetitive injuries, the real issue is one of trust: *Can I really trust that this will not happen again?*

Kristin shared with us how she had been repeatedly hurt by some things her boyfriend had done. This was a "pattern wound." Soon her self-protective instincts kicked in, and she became a little guarded when she was around him. Consequently, this cool distance began to irritate the guy. In an attempt to place some pressure on her, he simply asked when she was going to "get over" her hurt.

Kristin's response was classic: "I'll 'get over it' when you stop hurting me," she told him. "But until you do, it's like you just keep reinjuring the same old wound."

Trust is the foundation of any relationship. When Kristin realized she could not trust Steve not to hurt her again, she knew it was time to end it.

4. *When there are obvious relational problems*

Some problems in relationships are easy for you to see. Even if they are being hidden from everyone else, at least you are aware that something's not right. One example would be problems with abuse. This could be as blatant as physical abuse, where your boyfriend actually strikes you or threatens you with violence, or as subtle as emotional or verbal abuse. Either way, this controlling behavior represents an obvious problem within your boyfriend and for your relationship. Other examples of obvious problems would include things like extreme insensitivity to your legitimate needs, chronic bickering over little matters, or repeated disrespect.

In a caring relationship, it's easy to overlook some things—to cut your boyfriend a little slack. That's not all bad. We can all use a little grace. But grace can be taken to an unhealthy extreme. When trying to figure out where to draw the line on grace, ask the question, Is this an *incident* or a *pattern*? As we discussed earlier, an incident is something that occurs once or rarely. (There are some behaviors where even once is too much.) With most behaviors, we are not concerned with an isolated incident. But patterns—repetitive acts—are another matter. Negative patterns must be reckoned with and not simply overlooked.

5. *When either of you has significant personal problems*

I spent some time earlier identifying the kinds of things that constitute significant personal problems (see chapter 4). I want to remind you now of two things you need to understand as you make decisions about your relationship.

You will be influenced. Even though your boyfriend's personal problem is technically *his* responsibility, you, too, will be significantly influenced. That's because relationships are *cooperative* ventures. The whole point of being in a relationship is to form an interdependency. For good or for bad, you are influenced by everything that takes place. So don't naively think his problem won't become your problem. At some level, it will!

Only act on what you know to be true. No question about it, the personal problem may get better. Just because he's not marriage material right now doesn't mean he won't become marriage material in the future. So you may choose to give your situation a little time. Pray for your boyfriend; provide appropriate emotional support, and hold out for a change to occur. But don't be foolish. Lovedecisions are made on facts, not hopes. And sometimes the facts tell you—even when your heart may not— that it is time to let him go.

6. *You recognize that one of you isn't ready for marriage*

I like the term *readiness* because it capsulizes a number of problems. When associated with lovedecisions, it refers to the failure to meet some basic prerequisite to marriage. For example, if you have not yet "left home," then you are not ready to be married. This was the case with Penny.

I had seen Penny in counseling regarding some personal issues. During the counseling process it had become clear that Penny's mother was having a hard time letting her go. By the way Penny kept complying with all of her mother's demands, it had become equally clear that Penny was also having a difficult time making the break. Before returning home for the summer break, Penny told me she had gotten engaged. The date was set for the end of the next school year, and the wedding would be in Nashville instead of in her home church several hundred miles away. Nashville had become her home. She attended a church here, would begin her career here, and it was a more accessible location for all her friends. To no one's surprise, her mother was disappointed in this decision; she wanted the wedding to take place "at home."

I agreed to do the couple's premarital counseling when they returned for school in the fall but gave Penny this piece of advice to jump-start the process right away: "You're going to have to do a better job of leaving home before you can even think about getting married. You can do some of that work while you're home this summer." Penny understood what I was saying and left for home intending to establish some boundaries with her mother. When she returned to school that fall, the place of the wedding had been changed. It was now (to Penny's dismay) to take place in her hometown. Apparently she hadn't gotten much "work" done over the summer. Mom was still calling the shots. And Penny wasn't any "readier" for marriage than she had been when she'd left.

I'm not suggesting there is a right or wrong answer when you're deciding where to get married. I'm only describing the process that needs to be employed to get to that decision. Who really made the decision in this scenario? And what does that say about both Penny's ability to leave home and her readiness for marriage?

Sometimes readiness can pertain to personality issues. Maturity, for example, is a process requiring time and experience. Most of us eventually get there. But if there's been too little time or too little experience, chances are that an acceptable level of maturity may still be a way off. Immaturity might not be a lifelong trait, but it's definitely not the way to start a marriage. At other times, readiness may refer to circumstances. Not having a job to support the marriage is an example of a circumstance that may indicate the two of you aren't ready. The thought that you can "live on love" sounds romantic, but it's not the way the world works. Planning to be supported by your parents? Yikes! That's a disastrous circumstance. If that's what you're planning, you're not ready to marry.

7. *You recognize that the proposed marriage is not God's will*

I have chosen to talk about this indicator last, but in assessing your lovedecisions, it should be at the top of your list. It's always uncomfortable to offer advice to others about what God is saying for them to do—seems a little presumptuous to me. Still, there is one admonition that I feel pretty safe in making—the one that says you should not be "unequally yoked" (2 Corinthians 6:14 KJV). In other words, Christians should not marry non-Christians.

God has a good reason for giving us this relational guideline. To summarize a whole lot of examples and research: These marriages don't work. In this case *a* difference becomes *the* difference as many of these marriages end in divorce. And for those couples who do stay together, the influence of the non-believing partner has a tremendous impact on both the spiritual life of the believer and the intimacy level of the couple. It will create a distance in the relationship that may never be resolved. That's not what God had in mind when He created marriage. And for a Christian, without that spiritual connection your marriage will never be complete . . . never quite whole.

HOW DOES YOUR RELATIONSHIP COMPARE?

Although love is an essential part of any lovedecision, I think we've proven here that it's not the only part. How did your relationship compare against these indicators? If any of these examples caused you even a moment's reflection on your own personal circumstances, then look again. It may be time for you to cast a more serious eye toward what you really have.

14

Breaking Up Is Hard to Do

To: Paige@AlmostGraduated.com
From: Dad@HarveyHome.com
Subject: Kelli

Dear Paige,

Sounds like you've got a lot on your plate. In addition to school, work, and leading a pretty active social life, you've now taken on the role of personal counselor to your friend, Kelli. I applaud your compassion. That's probably a role that we all get into from time to time with our friends, and from what you say, she definitely needs someone to play that role with her now.

As you both have figured out, Kelli is in a difficult relationship. (I don't remember your mentioning her boyfriend's name in our conversation, but I'm probably safe in assuming it's not "the Jerk.") He sounds at least insensitive—if not a whole lot more. Kelli's decision to break off this relationship

To: Paige@AlmostGraduated.com
From: Dad@HarveyHome.com
Subject: Kelli

is wise on her part. But I suspect she may have a harder time following through on her decision than either of you expects.

Deciding to end a relationship is difficult enough. But actually going through with it has its own set of problems. You may find your role of counselor and friend to be difficult for a while. It's hard to watch someone you care about be mistreated. And you will wonder why in the world she doesn't just do something. Just remember: Things are always more complicated than they appear, and lots of things can interfere with our doing what we need to do.

I'd suggest that you just keep on being her friend. She needs someone stable in her life right now, and you seem to be offering her a safe place to vent. Support her in the constructive things she's trying to do and let her know she's not crazy. Her boyfriend will try to convince her otherwise. Most importantly, continue to pray for Kelli.

To: Paige@AlmostGraduated.com
From: Dad@HarveyHome.com
Subject: Kelli

You may become frustrated with what may appear to be inactivity on her part. But don't let that interfere with your continuing to be a friend. People usually do what they are "ready" to do. And in being a friend to Kelli, you are helping her more than you know to begin to take control of her life. If anything's going to get done, it's going to be because she does it—and not you.

Keep up the good work—and continue to be a friend to your friend.

I am ever amazed at your compassion for others.

Dad

THE NEXT STEP

You've decided you should end your relationship. But now comes the really hard part: doing it. Breaking up is sometimes so difficult that the people in the unsuccessful relationship stay in it even when they know it's not the right thing to do. Why is it so hard to break up? What stops you from doing what you know you need to do? That's the challenge we'll focus on in this chapter.

THE MOST COMMON REASONS FOR FAILING TO END A RELATIONSHIP (WHEN IT SHOULD BE ENDED)

Breaking up is never easy. If you've decided that's the best decision you can make right now, it's important to look at what might interfere with your process. By knowing some of the obstacles that may arise, you'll be better prepared to deal with them.

Before I get into my list of possibilities, I want you to recognize a great truth when it comes to breaking off relationships: There's not just one—and only one—reason that makes breaking it off difficult. Breaking up is not a simple problem, and the reasons for failing to do so are multiple. What hinders you may not be what hinders someone else. There are so many possible obstacles that I can't begin to include them all in this chapter. But there are some that seem to occur so often I can call them "common." Those are the ones I'll address in this section.

Reason 1: Experiencing outside pressure

One common complaint that I hear is, "This is what everyone wants me to do." I spoke to a girl recently who was engaged to a guy, and though she loved him, she questioned whether she had a marrying kind of love. The closer she got to the wedding, the more anxious she became. She finally decided she and her fiancé shouldn't get married, but she just couldn't break it off. Why? Because she didn't want to disappoint her parents. "Jeff has become the son they never had," she said. "I think they may even love him more than they do me!" She was in a tough spot. Was she going to disappoint her parents—or herself?

The pressure to not disappoint others also includes your friends. When friends say things like, "When are you guys going to get married? You're so right for each other," or "What are you waiting on? You know you're in love—go for it!" that puts pressure on you to stay in a relationship you might otherwise exit.

Sometimes this outside pressure comes in the form of special circumstances. "I'm already so 'obligated' it's too late to break it off," a bride-to-be might say. This usually means you've already spent some money. Weddings are expensive, and a lot of money goes out long before the ceremony takes place (invitations, bride and bridesmaids dresses, deposits for the honeymoon, etc.). But continuing into a marriage simply because of money is pretty shortsighted.

Being too concerned about what others might think can also be a big issue. It's common to hear someone say, "It would be too embarrassing to call it off." That reminds me of the wedding "dis-invitation" we got in the mail. It simply read, "The wedding between Jane Jones and John Smith will not occur." That couple obviously believed a little short-term embarrassment was better than long-term turmoil.

What do these situations have in common? Simply this: When it comes to a relationship, you have to determine whose needs are more important—the people on the outside or the people on the inside. That should be a no-brainer.

Reason 2: Taking on too much responsibility

The complaint I hear that tells me you're taking on too much responsibility is, "I don't want to hurt his feelings." There are some similarities between feeling pressure from parents and from your boyfriend. Both are instances where you are wrestling with the fear of disappointing someone. But I list concern for your boyfriend's feelings separately from family and friends' feelings because "disappointment" doesn't really capture the depth of the emotion here. When it comes to romantic involvements, your real concern is, *How much is this going to hurt him?*

Failing to do what you need to do because you fear hurting his feelings is an example of boundary confusion. Boundaries are those emotional lines that separate people. In this case, you've confused what you are and are not responsible for. When it gets down to it, you are only responsible for honestly dealing with *your* stuff—how *you* feel. I'm not saying that you can't be concerned about how your boyfriend feels. You're not cold and callous. And it isn't your goal to go out of your way to hurt him. But neither do you want to be deceptive. Your goal is honesty—with yourself and your boyfriend. And sometimes, in your effort to be honest, feelings will get hurt.

Reason 3: Wanting to avoid the emotional hassle of breaking up

Taking on too much responsibility means you're overprotecting him. When you know you should break up but you don't because you're avoiding the emotional hassle, your concern has shifted. Now you are overprotecting yourself. This is when I hear statements like, "It's going to hurt too much," and "It's just too much trouble to end it."

I was talking with a group of single adults about the difficulties of breaking up when one of them blurted out, "Oh, man, I just don't look forward to all the crying we're both going to do. It's just too hard!" His statement caught everyone off guard. But after a few chuckles, heads started to nod, and "Boy, isn't that the truth" began to echo around the room.

No doubt about it. Getting out of a relationship is a hassle. And some of the hassle is the emotional pain you're going to feel. The truth is that relationships are easier to get into than they are to get out of. That's why we sometimes stay in them longer than we should. Wanting to avoid emotional pain is normal. I don't know anyone who likes crying so much that he or she looks forward to breaking up for the sheer enjoyment of it! But letting fear control your decisions only makes life harder. You're going to hurt. But you will survive, and you will heal, and you will move on with your life. So face your fear of pain and get on with the healing.

Reason 4: Fear of what you're losing

Fear of losing something comes in a couple of different variations. First there is the fear of losing all you've invested. This person might say, "Breaking up means starting over with nothing and losing all that other stuff." I met with a girl who had been in a two-and-a-half-year relationship, and according to her calculations that was six months too long. But she was having a hard time letting go. "I should be gone," she said. "But it's so hard. I look at all the time I've invested—all of it will be wasted if we break up! And I'll have to start over with someone else and maybe get to the same place in that relationship that I am now in this one."

Not wanting to lose what you've got is a common theme. Sometimes it's expressed in terms as though you're losing an investment and feeling hesitant to start over in another relationship. At other times it's expressed more as a loss of identity. Being in a relationship defines you as a couple and may sound better than being labeled as a single. "Couple-hood" might be a difficult status for you to give up. Maybe it's got more to do with comfort and security. Being in a relationship is more predictable than wondering if someone will ask you out or not. Or maybe you've already become a part of the "fam." He can go, but you just can't stand the thought of losing his parents (or sisters, etc.).

The fear of losing all that other "stuff" can get in the way of making a good decision. But when you get down to it, marriage isn't about that other stuff anyway. It's about two people—two people who need to be right for each other. And if you're not right for each other, there's not enough other stuff to ever correct it.

Reason 5: Wanting marriage to redeem your mistakes

Two wrongs don't make a right. That's a rule that was taught to us by our mothers and then reinforced by our kindergarten and Sunday school teachers. With all that instruction, you'd think we would have learned it. But just because something's been *taught* doesn't mean it's been *caught*. And some of us are real slow learners. I see examples of this "slow learning" time and time again in relationships. It happens when we believe, "Marriage will make things right" and then try to correct something we've done by marrying the person with whom we've done it.

The most common example of trying to make something right with two wrongs is when couples try to use marriage to correct their sexual history. Maybe they didn't intend to become sexually active, but passion just overcame them. Or maybe they rationalized that they were planning to get married anyway so what was the harm in acting like they already had? Whatever the intent or plan that got them into their mess, things changed between them. Now, with the passion of infatuation waning, or the fantasized prince finally being seen as the toad that he is, or any number of other reasons, one or both partners question whether marriage is really what they want. Yet what other choice do they have? Their behavior in this relationship will now have implications for any future relationships. So they reason that they might as well get married and "fix it."

I don't think so! Two wrongs *don't* make a right.

I'm not saying that two people who have been sexually active shouldn't ever get married. Or that a couple who find themselves pregnant shouldn't consider marriage. But marriage should never be seen as a solution for a bad history. It must be decided upon on its own merits. God always has a future for His people, and there's no past He can't redeem. It's always best to place our past and our future in His hands instead of trying to do something with either one on our own.

Reason 6: Marriage as a rescue

Some people have the attitude, "Marriage will fix what's wrong with me and my life." Marriage is a relationship—not a life preserver—and you don't want to get those two confused. In the film *Jerry McGuire* actor Tom Cruise made famous the line, "You complete me." It was a touching scene, and there's a hint of truth in what he said. Relationships are made up of two individuals who become interdependent: Each develops a partial reliance upon the other. But when you look to another person to really "complete" you—to make you feel fulfilled or happy or to give you a sense of purpose or definition as a person—you are expecting too much. Personal fulfillment, happiness, purpose, and identity are the things you accomplish on your own. A healthy marriage begins with two *whole* people. If you're not happy before you get married, not much will change after you get married. You will still be unhappy. Marriage will not rescue you from your unhappiness with who you are.

Neither will marriage rescue you from your unhappiness with the circumstances in your life. I had a client who said all she wanted out of marriage was a chance to be "a kept woman." She was tired of the struggle to support herself and was ready for someone else to take on that job. Another client saw marriage as a way of escaping an abusive home and family. "I want someone to take me away from this mess," she said.

Marriage can definitely change the circumstances in your life. It can affect your income. It can make it possible for you to not work (though often it doesn't). It will change your living arrangements and can change your connections to family. But these factors also can be changed without getting married and probably need to if they are problems for you. Whatever the case, these changes in your circumstances should always be seen as the *consequences* of your decision to marry and never as the *reasons* for that decision.

MAKING ADULT DECISIONS

There's no right reason for doing the wrong thing—and proceeding in a relationship that needs to end is wrong. Part of growing up is taking on more and more responsibility for yourself. So if you know what you need to do, maybe it's time to face whatever it is that's causing your interference and act like an adult.

PART 4

THE SPIRITUAL SIDE OF
LOVE AND RELATIONSHIPS

15

Be What You Want to Find

To: Paige@JobSearch.com
From: Dad@HarveyHome.com
Subject: Don and Jamie

Dear Paige,

Don and Jamie came to my relationships 101 class today and shared some of their dating history. You know how candid they can be. In their "early years," Don wasn't a Christian. That "unequally yoked" dynamic always makes for interesting class discussion, and the students seemed to know exactly what Don and Jamie were talking about.

Though I've known Don and Jamie since before they were married, I always learn something new about them when they come to one of my classes. What struck me today was something that Jamie first mentioned and then Don echoed—her gradual spiritual decline as a result of being

To: Paige@JobSearch.com
From: Dad@HarveyHome.com
Subject: Don and Jamie

with Don—and what it ultimately meant for them as a twosome. It was interesting that Don also noticed this subtle change while they were dating.

Jamie described her efforts at "trying to live in two different worlds"—trying to "tack" Christianity onto the rest of her life. It was funny to hear her describe the conversation she had with her mother "over and over again" and the "trite" phrases that both she and her mother used. The conversation would go something like this:

"Jamie, you don't need to be dating someone who isn't a Christian."

"Mother, I'm only dating him. I'm not going to marry him."

"Jamie, you only fall in love with the people you date."

"Mother, I'm not going to fall in love with someone who isn't a Christian. I'm just having fun! I might even influence his life."

To: Paige@JobSearch.com
From: Dad@HarveyHome.com
Subject: Don and Jamie

But she did fall in love with Don. And though she remained a Christian throughout their relationship, Jamie admitted that it cost her her spiritual edge. This happened when she compromised her values. Jamie used one set of values when she was around her Christian friends and another when she was around Don's. Compromising always comes with a price.

Then, when Don became a Christian, Jamie thought their relationship would really take off. But just the opposite occurred. Don was completely committed. He gave up all his old friends. He knew he couldn't just tack his new faith onto a worldly lifestyle. And even though Jamie had been a Christian all along, the rules that had governed their relationship when Don was not a Christian still hung around. They tried, but they couldn't seem to make the adjustment. So even though they still cared for each other, they ended the relationship.

I guess their story could have ended with

To: Paige@JobSearch.com
From: Dad@HarveyHome.com
Subject: Don and Jamie

their breakup, but it didn't. A lot of personal and spiritual growth took place over the next two years. Their getting back together was a real surprise to many of their friends, but no one was more surprised than Don and Jamie. This "new" relationship had a different set of rules. Being "equally yoked" really worked.

It's nice to see a story end well. Not all of them do. I know how much you think of Jamie and Don, so I wanted to share a little of their journey with you. There's a lot that can be learned from the experiences of others. Hopefully these experiences help cement the truths of God's Word and His great love for us into our souls.

With a growing confidence in your judgment,

Dad

WHERE, HOW, WHAT — AND OTHER
"FIRST GRADE" WORDS

I had been counseling with John and Joan for several weeks. About halfway through one of our sessions, John unexpectedly asked me how I thought his marriage compared with the marriages of other couples I counsel. John was looking for a way to evaluate his and Joan's relationship. Were they better off than most of my clients? Were they worse off? Exactly where did they fall?

Where a couple is in their relationship—how healthy they are as individuals and as a couple—has a lot to do with what we can do in therapy. But to me, something more important than "where" they are is the direction they're heading. So I decided to answer John's question with a metaphor; I began talking about elevators.

"How do you and Joan get to my office?" My private therapy practice is situated in an office building near downtown Nashville. It's got a great view of a park and a large university campus. Though these are the positives, it also has some negatives. For example, do not try to climb the stairs to my office! I'm located on the tenth floor, and the trek through the stairwell can be exhausting. My clients don't use the stairs; they take one of three elevators. Above each elevator is a digital device that indicates which floor the elevator is currently stopped on. So if elevator number one is on the fifth floor, the digital indicator will flash "5."

New clients on their way to my office (and those who aren't real elevator savvy), often stand back and simply wait for one of the elevator's doors to open. They may not even notice there are numbers above the doors. Others look at the digital indicators and move toward the elevator that seems to be on the floor closest to the lobby. But the more sophisticated elevator users move toward an elevator after watching the digital indicators to determine *which direction* each elevator is moving—up or down. They have learned that direction is more important than location.

So how did I respond to John's original question of how his marriage compared to the other couples I counsel? After talking about elevators and how he and Joan had gotten to my office, I told them that how they compare to other couples isn't the important issue. What is important is the direction in which their relationship is moving. Are their problems getting better? Are they getting worse? Or is there no change at all? "The direction in which you're moving is much more important than where your relationship was when you first came in for counseling," I told them.

TRENDS AND PATTERNS

Direction is always more important than location. That's something too many people in the lovedecisions phase of life don't always understand. For example, I see a lot of young singles asking questions like, "How far can I go and still remain a Christian?" "At what point does my sexual behavior become sin?" "I'm *in* the world, but when is it that I become *of* the world?" (See John 17:15–16.) These are "directional" questions. And if you're asking these kinds of questions, you're already missing the point. These questions are concerned with how far you can get from God, not with how close you can draw near to Him.

Over the past few years, I've been on several Christian

campuses, and in talking with students I've become aware of some common dating behaviors. Though known by many different names, one of these is "messing around." You know . . . not having sex, per se, but coming as close as you can and stopping just short of intercourse. When I ask how they handle what some would see as a contradiction—being a Christian yet behaving very sexually—the answer I get is, "If we weren't Christian, we'd just have sex. But since we are Christian, we don't. We're just messing around—and the Bible doesn't say anything about that." At best, this is "directional" behavior.

Imagine for a moment that you have drawn a large circle on the ground and are standing somewhere inside the ring. Now place God inside the ring with you. In fact, let's place Him in the exact center of the circle. For the purpose of our illustration, anything inside the circle is Christian. You may be close to the center, or you may be far from the center, but as long as you are in the circle, you are in a relationship with God. Contrarily, anything outside the circle is of the world. Your direction is simple to determine. Look at your behavior. Is what you're doing moving you toward the Savior (toward the center) or away from Him (toward the edge)?

The world is alluring—even inviting. But you think, *I don't dare cross over the line.* So, if you are interested in having a piece of both worlds, what do you do? You move as close to the edge of the circle as possible. You may even lean over the edge a little. But you're very careful because you don't want to accidentally cross the line and leave your Christian life behind. At least that's your reasoning. You think it's OK to get closer and closer to the world. Just keep at least one foot in the circle. This is "directional" thinking.

If you hold to the belief that *where* you are is the most important issue—that as long as you are somewhere in the circle then everything is OK—then you don't have any problem with marginal behavior. You can tack Christianity onto a worldly lifestyle, or compartmentalize your life, or mix and match your standards. You can praise God one night and mess around the next. But if you accept the notion that direction is also important, you are suddenly faced with a dilemma, because directionally, when you are moving toward the edge of the circle, you are moving away from the center. In this illustration, that means you are moving away from God, and moving away from God is never a good thing to do.

Moving away from God is what Jamie did when she first attempted to include Don in her life. Jamie was still in the circle, and she didn't see herself as intentionally moving away from God. She just saw herself as moving *toward* Don. But the result was the same. Jamie had divided her life into two compartments—Christian living and non-Christian living. She knew what Scripture said about being "unequally yoked" (see 2 Corinthians 6:14 KJV), but by compartmentalizing, she was able to rationalize away the contradiction. She told herself, *I'm not going to marry Don. I'm only dating him—having some fun.* So Jamie moved toward the edge, and for a while had what she wanted: She stayed in the circle *and* had Don. But there are always consequences to the choices we make. And for Jamie, the cost was her spiritual edge.

WHAT IS IT YOU REALLY WANT IN A LIFE PARTNER?

The words of Solomon have withstood the test of time: "There is nothing new under the sun" (Ecclesiastes 1:9). In youth-talk this means, "Been there—done that." It's all happened before. That's true with the tendency to compartmentalize your life. It doesn't take an investigator to uncover historical examples of compartmentalizing. All you have to do is read the daily newspaper. We know presidents who have lied, church leaders who have had mistresses, and police officers who have broken the law. What is new is the prevalence and ease with which this kind of behavior now occurs. We are living in a time when compartmentalizing is almost the norm. But "everybody's doing it" still doesn't make it right—and it doesn't get you what you really want.

How do I know that? Because I ask. When I talk with young Christian singles who are in the process of making lovedecisions, I ask, "What do you want in a life partner?" I consistently hear the same description: "I want someone who will genuinely love me and who has a heart for God." Yet amazingly, this is not who these singles necessarily tend to date—nor is it who they tend to *be*. They will date the "Dons" of this world, just wanting to "have some fun." And behaving in this compartmentalized manner—staying in the circle but moving as close to the edge as they can—tells me something about who they are.

What's wrong with this picture?! And to top it off, they still expect to find their Mr. Right—someone with a heart for God. This is crazy thinking. You're not going to find a life partner with a heart for God by dating guys who don't have a heart for God. That's like expecting to find feathers in a cuckoo clock. Get real!

IT'S TIME FOR A LITTLE SELF-ASSESSMENT

Let's look at *your* behavior and see what it's telling us about your life plan and your own spirituality.

Your life plan

I'll get a little presumptuous here and assume your life plan is like most of the other Christian singles I talk with, that you want to marry a spiritual guy. If you're not dating this kind of guy, what does that tell you about the life you're living and the direction you're leaning? Is it confusing for you? Is it taking away your spiritual edge? And what is it communicating to others? Dating is a two-way street, you know. What makes you think you can live life on the edge—self-absorbed and leaning toward the world—and still end up with a spiritually mature and sensitive man? Hey, if he's all that spiritually mature, what is there about you that he's supposed to find desirable? Don't you think he can figure out which direction you're moving?

Your own spiritual life

If we strip away the rationalizing and the excuses, what is your behavior telling you about your own spiritual life? Have you been fooling yourself? Where is your heart? If your behavior has you moving away from God, maybe that's showing you something about yourself that you need to deal with. Sure, you want to end up with someone spiritually mature, but is that who *you* really are? Maybe there's a reason why you are attracted to marginal guys. Denying reality may make you feel more comfortable—but it doesn't change anything. If you're moving away from God, then you're moving away from God. Reality's what *is*. Guard your heart.

BE WHAT YOU WANT TO FIND

Finding a life partner is a two-vote situation. If what you want in a mate is someone who has a heart for God, then this is the kind of person you need to date—and this is the kind of person you need to be. Don't fool yourself and think you can end up with this kind of relationship by either dating someone who isn't—or being someone who isn't. When it comes to finding a godly life partner, there are three prerequisites:

- Know what you want.

- Be true to God.

- Be what you want to find.

16

True Intimacy: God's Best for Your Sex Life

To: Paige@OnMyOwn.com
From: Dad@HarveyHome.com
Subject: Sex

Dear Paige,

It was good to hear your voice last night, even if it was just over the phone. At this stage in life, I'm glad for even these brief encounters with my girl. Though I'm glad to hear how well things are going in your life, it hurts me to hear how difficult things are for Heather and Aaron. I know you've been their friend since you were a freshman in college. Didn't you even give up some of your last summer of freedom in order to be in their wedding? For them to be having marital difficulty this early really isn't a good sign.

I know you're closer to Heather than to Aaron so you're probably only getting one side of the situation, but still, what she's

To: Paige@OnMyOwn.com
From: Dad@HarveyHome.com
Subject: Sex

telling you seems to make a lot of sense. Her admitting that they had become sexually active early in their dating relationship makes her other complaints almost predictable—complaints that their relationship has seemed to stop growing, that they really don't know each other now, and that they find it difficult to feel passionate anymore. These are some of the common consequences that usually occur when couples get things out of order.

We are sexual beings. That's the way God created us. And sex plays a big part in our feeling emotionally close and fulfilled in marriage. But His design comes with instructions, and these directions include an order in which things are to occur—an order the world has tried to change. God's design is marriage before sex; the world's design is sex before marriage. And although society will continue to try and convince us its way is the right one and God's is wrong, remember: God is not arbitrary. He never

To: Paige@OnMyOwn.com
From: Dad@HarveyHome.com
Subject: Sex

tells us to do anything that isn't in our best interest. And that's especially true with sex.

I know there are a lot of spiritual reasons for following God's timetable, and these reasons are important. But there are a lot of relational reasons as well. Heather and Aaron's marital problems are an example of what can happen when you mess up a relationship with sex. So, as hard as it is for a friend to watch another friend suffer, I guess there's a lesson to be learned here. It's OK to be passionate about one another. But it's very important to know your limits and to establish your boundaries. That's the only way you'll experience true intimacy in any relationship. So, Paige, keep your life and your heart pure—and you'll experience God's best.

All my love,

Dad

I recently counseled a non-Christian couple who had started having sex one month into their dating relationship. After several months of engagement and a couple of months of marriage, they came in because they "couldn't relate anymore." They had used sex as the way to resolve all their conflicts and to express and validate their feelings. After the sexual excitement had waned somewhat, they realized they hadn't done much in the way of building real emotional intimacy. As I described what premature sex does to pollute relationship building, the wife responded, "Why doesn't anybody ever tell you this stuff?" This chapter is an attempt to tell you this "stuff" so you can inherit God's promises rather than unnecessary pain.

Most churched young adults know that sex before marriage is forbidden scripturally, but they want to know the practical reasons for abstaining. Our culture certainly doesn't endorse waiting. In fact, it's not uncommon for the world to laugh at abstinence. The '60s and '70s saw our culture take sex out of marriage. The '80s saw us take sex out of serious relationships; and in the '90s and the new millennium, we have taken sex out of relationships and into recreation—casual sex. The prevailing attitude seems to be, "I have needs; what's the big deal?" The truisms of that last sentence are that yes, we have needs, and yes, premarital sex is a big deal.

The problem for many of you may be this: The information I'm going to present in this chapter may come too late. You may have already experienced sex and have been so influenced by this culture, it may be easy for you to minimize or not recognize the emotional consequences you'll experience now and in your future marriage. Or it may be that the consequences you've experienced are also physical and you are suffering with the pain and shame of a sexually transmitted disease. Or maybe you've had a pregnancy and possibly even an abortion. Or the sexual experience could have occurred in the form of abuse, and you are struggling with healing from that pain. Wherever you are regarding your sexual experience, this chapter is all about knowing emotional health—either maintaining it or reclaiming it. The decision is yours. So here's some of the data you'll need to know to make a decision for emotional health.

THE POSITIVE SIDE OF DATING

First of all, dating is a good thing. Keep it up! Dating gives you the opportunity to mature and discover who you are and whom you want to partner with for the rest of your life. Positive dating relationships help you develop the skills and goals that center around developing your identity. Having a good sense of who you are and where you place your boundaries prepares you to move into your mid- to late twenties, when the developmental goal will be for you to establish intimacy with one other person. There are no shortcuts to wholeness as a person, but there are several things that can interfere. Premature sex is one of them.

When you are in a dating relationship and choose to wait for sex until marriage, you learn to delay gratification, which is a mandatory personality characteristic for maturity. It's also an integral part of a healthy marriage because healthy marriage relationships are all about doing what's best for the other person. Someone who can't sacrifice for you now probably won't do it later, either. Marriage requires a lot of mutual sacrifice. Never marry a selfish person! Self-gratification is all about what meets "my" need—not the other person's needs, and not the relationship's needs.

DEVELOPING SENSITIVITY IN YOUR BOYFRIEND

If you want a husband who can be understanding and emotionally supportive of you after you're married, now is the time to develop that pattern. The healthy way to do that is to develop good communication and conflict-resolution patterns now because, remember, what *is,* will *be.* Couples who can communicate well and resolve conflicts efficiently are the ones who can make a marriage work. This is not an easy endeavor, but it can be fun. It can even be some of the best parts of being in a serious relationship. Denying sex in dating forces you both to focus on developing relationship skills that are an absolute necessity for a good marriage. A guy who has learned to deal with conflict, instead of avoid it, has learned to identify and be assertive with his feelings, and has learned to hear and respond to your heart's needs. That's the kind of guy who could consistently be the love of your life, right?

Love does promote a sexual energy that provides a motivation to learn all you can about each other. But sex before marriage throws up a big stop sign to intimacy development between the two of you. Why is that? The truth is, once sex has begun, the focus of the relationship turns from learning about one another and what each of you needs emotionally, to how to strategize the next date so that sex is available. Respect for one another is diminished, and motivation to work on the relationship wanes.

Setting the pace of your physical involvement now can't guarantee an emotionally sensitive spouse, but it can go a long way in preventing an insensitive one. That's a pretty bold statement, I realize, but let me explain. In our culture, many guys weren't brought up to be sensitive to emotions. Some wonderful moms and dads validated their little boys' feelings and taught them to relate to others' feelings and respond appropriately. Many didn't. Instead they taught their little boys to be tough and courageous, which often seemed at odds with sensitivity. Many guys didn't grow up learning to identify and discuss their feelings. Therefore they now struggle with the ability to express them. These fellas are more comfortable with expressing their emotions through their behavior.

Women, however, crave tenderness, touching, talking, and expressing love through words. (Why do you think romance novels are so popular?) And many men are ill-equipped to meet that need. For many guys, sex is a substitute for emotional expression—for sharing. It's a substitute for intimacy, especially for those guys who don't know how to develop the real thing. Real intimacy puts demands on the two of you: talking and sharing your emotions, your dreams, sharing who you are deep within. And it requires a genuine mutual understanding between the two of you. It's a rather complicated process that requires time and the mutual desire to know the other person and his or her needs. If you accept a substitute for that process through sex, not only have you halted the momentum of intimacy, but you may not ever get it going again.

WE ARE SEXUAL BEINGS

Sex is God's turf! He created it. He values it so much He uses it as His analogy for the deep level of love and commitment Christ has for the church, His bride (see Revelation 21:9 and Matthew 9:15). It's a holy thing to Him. We are created to be sexual beings, to desire that type of closeness and commitment to one other person in the world.

What was God's purpose? I believe He needed to give us a way to communicate love that encompassed every aspect of our being—physical, emotional, spiritual, and relational. Wholesome relational sex is a means of communicating the depth of your love commitment to your spouse in a way that language alone can't accomplish. It is God's provision for completeness—a final signature on the marital covenant. Sex is a covenant act. When you have sex you are saying, *I will never love another; my covenant is with you.* It is the seal of oneness. And a covenant without commitment is a lie.

Since we are sexual, sensual beings, waiting to have sex until marriage is often a challenge—especially in this media-engulfed culture where the focus of every sitcom seems to be around the goal of jumping into bed. When I talk to college students, even on a Christian campus, many are caught up in rationalizing a way to somehow make sexuality before marriage OK. Or they define sex as being intercourse alone and then rationalize that "everything else" is acceptable to God. Of course, rationalizing is a coping mechanism that allows us to accept something we don't really believe to be acceptable. The outcome is that in order to reduce our anxiety as Christians, some young women compartmentalize their lives. Since God biblically tells us not to give our bodies to another outside of marriage ("Flee from sexual immorality" is not an unclear statement [1 Corinthians 6:18 NIV]. *Flee* means "to run in terror"), they attempt to mentally keep their spiritual life separate from their romantic life and actions.

When you trust in the words of your friends and/or the media over the words of your God, you are deceiving yourself. The rationalizing doesn't hold up. It will hold you together temporarily, but Jesus through the Holy Spirit has a pesky way of integrating us into one whole person. When we really ask His opinion, He convicts us of our sin and shows us that we are to be whole. That means there's no place for secret compartments. And then it simply becomes an issue of obedience.

So the question becomes, If I am a sexual being with normal desires and trying to obey God in this area, how do I keep myself honest sexually? The answer is (1) you *talk* about it with your boyfriend, and (2) you make plans that avoid risky situations. You talk about your feelings and your boundaries. You know, animals don't have the advantage of language. They have to resort to behaviors to communicate. Thank goodness we're more advanced than animals and we can communicate with words! Speaking honestly with the one you love is giving a great gift to that person. Telling your boyfriend you are attracted to him and desire him is very affirming. To also tell him that you care about yourself and your future husband enough to protect your future marriage relationship is also affirming to him that you are a person of substance. No matter what your boyfriend might say in a passionate moment, he admires that.

Also, to keep yourself honest sexually you need to make plans to avoid risky situations—and you make them on Monday, not on Saturday night. Your virginity, or born-again virginity, is something to protect because it will be your best wedding gift one day. Set boundaries on where you will go and what you will do, and don't get more passionate physically than you are comfortable with. I can't dictate for you where that "comfort" line is, but most counselors agree anything further than full-mouth kissing is too arousing.

A friend who is a prominent sex therapist said to me recently, "I am so angry at the fact that women today are being sold down the river when it comes to sexuality." She is saying that women often exchange their femininity for body exposure; their mystery is sacrificed for lust. Some women today find it helps them meet men if they wear certain blouses that show a little more than curves. I truly believe they *will* meet men that way. But what kind? Ladies, dress for the type of man you want to impress—someone who will notice your eyes and not your cleavage.

GOD'S DESIGN

Since God made us, He ought to know how to "run" us. Since He made us sexual, there must be a really good reason for Him to ask us to reserve sexual activity for that one person. After all, God's way provides not only sexual health, but emotional health.

I once heard an illustration of how Christians and non-Christians differ in their views of life. Non-Christians think Christians see life as a great green field with a few deep, muddy holes to be avoided. (Premarital sex is one of them.) They can plainly see that people who fall into these holes don't die. They don't even seem to be suffering many visible negative consequences. Therefore, the deduction is that Christianity is wrong. The reality is that Christians *do* see life as God made it—a beautiful green field. But we aren't frolicking across it avoiding the holes. We are already *in* the hole. In fact, because of sin, we were *born* in the hole. Only Jesus can provide us a way to escape the hole—clean off the mud and give us life. Sex before marriage keeps us in the muddy hole. God says, "I've got much better to offer you. I know you, and I know how to fulfill you, keep you safe, and make you unbelievably happy. Trust Me." God never offers you second best! With God, you never have to settle. You may have to wait, but you don't have to settle for second best.

God knows that once you're married you'll have to have ultimate trust in your husband to have a fulfilling sex life. How many of your best friends do you *not* trust? Most likely you'd say, "None." God created you to seek a trusting relationship with others. Think about it. The most basic element of all our relationships is trust. As a baby you learn whether or not the world is a safe place based on your parents' ability to meet your physical and emotional needs. You learn to trust, or not to trust. God's blueprint within your heart has designed you to seek close relationships with only those you can trust. True love is trustworthy because it comes with the God-given desire to protect the loved one.

Trust is essential for tender, relational sex in a marriage. When sex occurs outside of marriage, that love and protection most young women seek from their boyfriends is lost. With loss of protection comes the loss of trust for your best interest. Often you can't explain or even identify the problem, but the nagging question about whether his love is real haunts you. You want a guy who can delay having his own sexual needs met in order to have the best for his marriage. In fact, it's always a sign that your boyfriend does love you if he's able to respect your sexual boundaries. Love always respects, while lust has to have what it wants immediately and pouts or gets angry when denied. Remember, lust is always self-serving. Desire is normal, but if someone *demands* sex as an indication of your love, run! Or as the Bible says, *flee* in terror. That's lust—the counterfeit to love.

As a therapist, I work with many couples in pre-engagement and premarital counseling. Recently I counseled with a young couple who had dated for four years. The young woman just couldn't bring herself to commit to an engagement. After a few sessions we discussed their sexual relationship. They had engaged in sex for a while until she stopped it. She said she no longer felt like she was number one in his life and began to question his genuine love for her. She described her fear that he would not be faithful in marriage. All this came as a total surprise to her fiancé. He was confused.

As we discussed her deeper feelings, she was able to identify the lack of total trust that had arisen from their sexual encounters. Even though they both wanted to have sex at the time, the result was her feeling that his love was not protective, therefore not genuine. To engage in a covenant experience without a covenant commitment is a wound to your soul. And even though you can't put it into words, you feel the betrayal.

YOUR REAL NEED: CLOSENESS AND COMMUNICATION

A woman's sexual needs are far different from a man's. You need to feel emotionally close to your husband in order to desire and have fulfilling sex. You need to feel cherished—to feel "first" in his life. Solomon knew that when he fell in love with the Shulamite woman. He described her as being "altogether beautiful, . . . [without] blemish," one who "made my heart beat faster . . . with a single glance of your eyes" (Song of Solomon 4:7, 9 NASB). What woman wouldn't melt with that kind of love expressed? Women desire emotional closeness, and they feel this closeness through conversation, sharing, and feeling valued.

Sexually, women operate on two tracks: a physical track and an emotional track. Both have to be operating for good relational sex. The problem is that many young women confuse their physical desire for sexuality with their need for emotional closeness. So when the sex is over and their emotional needs are still not met, they are frustrated. Their answer to the frustration is to simply try again, when the reality is that they need to meet their need for emotional closeness and intimacy through loving communication with their boyfriend. Sex isn't a *remedy* for anything—loneliness, emotional needs, or better self-esteem. In fact, if you have a pretty low self-esteem, you are vulnerable to sexual attention from men. If you have a good sense of self and an established identity, it will be easier for you to set healthy boundaries.

In their book *Relationships*, Les and Leslie Parrot make a great statement: "If you try to find intimacy with another person before achieving a sense of identity on your own, all your relationships become an attempt to complete yourself." Becoming a healthy whole person is hard work. There are no shortcuts to wholeness. It comes only through one good decision after another. Remember, God's way equals emotional health.

SO HOW DO I GAIN BACK MY HEALTH?

A generation has sought to meet a valid need in an invalid way, and the consequences are disease, restlessness, divorce, and a lack of sexual responsiveness. When I was a child, my mom taught me to taste foods—really taste them—for quality and flavor. Now I cringe at preassembled microwave dishes. I can't eat that stuff, it's so saturated with synthetic flavor. Yet a generation is being taught through advertising that this is great food. And in the process, those youngsters are losing sight of what real food tastes like. They're missing out on the real thing, and they don't even know it. Their only hope is to be reintroduced to good food.

God wants to reintroduce you to wholeness. And only He can do it. If you've already experienced sex either willingly or unwillingly, God can still rebuild your emotional and sexual health. In Jeremiah 31:3–4 God said, "I have loved you with an everlasting love; I have drawn you with loving-kindness. I will build you up again and you will be rebuilt" (NIV).

There is such a thing as spiritual virginity. When I do pre-engagement or premarital counseling with Christian couples in which one or both have had sexual experiences, I talk with them about their need to feel like spiritual virgins with each other. I suggest that they, together, plan a ritual where they go perhaps to their church or another place that is sacred to them and that they bow before God and ask His forgiveness for the past and His cleansing for the future. Together they commit to each other to start fresh as God sees them—as spiritual virgins—and accept His newness.

From this comes a sense of freedom—a fresh slate. They commit to walk in protective love for each other, now and throughout life. You can do the same thing. The apostle Paul wrote, "It is for freedom that Christ has set us free. Stand firm, then, and do not let yourselves be burdened again by a yoke of slavery" (Galatians 5:1 NIV) The past is not your future. Celebrate!

17

Dear Dad

To: Dad@HarveyHome.com
From: Paige@OnMyOwn.com
Subject: Thank you!

Dear Dad,

When you told me you were going to write your next book to an audience of twenty-somethings, I was thrilled. Finally, the advice and insight you'd shared with me during my growing-up years was going to be made available to other "daughters" my age. I was flattered when you showed your confidence in my abilities by asking me to edit the manuscript before sending it to a "real editor." Sneaky. I know you often tell people that my dating life "kept you with plenty of content to write about." That was certainly evident as I received many of your sample chapters at very significant times in my life. And as I combed through your writing, chapter by chapter, there was more going on than just editing. While I was

To: Dad@HarveyHome.com
From: Paige@OnMyOwn.com
Subject: Thank you!

sifting out the clinical terms and misplaced apostrophes, the message became real to me. I began to feel the vision for the project.

Suddenly I became so much more aware of the relationships that surrounded me—friends, acquaintances, even people I did not know but watched from a distance—observable relationships that seemed to be on collision courses. I found myself wanting to share your choppy, unfinished manuscript with others in the lovedecisions phase. I wanted to point out the reasons why one couple might want to rethink their decision to marry, or to help my girlfriend identify controlling behavior in her boyfriend. However, I'm not the therapist, and I don't have the answers.

But I read a book that did—this one!

When I look back at the e-mails you've written me, I can see a time line of my own dating experiences as well as those of many of my friends. My confidence in making

To: Dad@HarveyHome.com
From: Paige@OnMyOwn.com
Subject: Thank you!

lovedecisions has become increasingly strong. It doesn't mean the decisions themselves have all been easy, but even at that, I realize I've made the right ones despite the difficulty that accompanied them. I wish I could give sole credit to my own wisdom and growing maturity, but we both know you've given me too many answers and explanations over the years for that to be true.

Thank you for always knowing what to say. And for always being right! It seems, lately, when I give you updates on my dating life, you do more listening than advising. I think that's a good sign. It means I can make these decisions confidently, knowing my eyes are wide open to the realities of what it means to make a healthy lovedecision.

Thank you for truly setting an example for healthy marriage with Mom. I can only hope that my own marriage will have characteristics that mirror yours—complete trust; honest and loyal communication with a

To: Dad@HarveyHome.com
From: Paige@OnMyOwn.com
Subject: Thank you!

sacrifice of pride; love most of all; and a shared intimacy with Christ. You can rest in the knowledge that I will not settle for someone who isn't my Mr. Right. I would cheat myself and my future with anything less. That is what you taught me. You did a good job.

Always your girl,

Paige